Spark™

Big Data Cluster Computing in Production

Spark™

Big Data Cluster Computing in Production

Ilya Ganelin
Ema Orhian
Kai Sasaki
Brennon York

WILEY

Spark™: Big Data Cluster Computing in Production

Published by
John Wiley & Sons, Inc.
10475 Crosspoint Boulevard
Indianapolis, IN 46256
www.wiley.com

Copyright © 2016 by John Wiley & Sons, Inc., Indianapolis, Indiana
Published simultaneously in Canada

ISBN: 978-1-119-25401-0

ISBN: 978-1-119-25404-1 (ebk)

ISBN: 978-1-119-25405-8 (ebk)

Manufactured in the United States of America

10 9 8 7 6 5 4 3 2 1

For general information on our other products and services please contact our Customer Care Department within the United States at (877) 762-2974, outside the United States at (317) 572-3993 or fax (317) 572-4002.

Wiley publishes in a variety of print and electronic formats and by print-on-demand. Some material included with standard print versions of this book may not be included in e-books or in print-on-demand. If this book refers to media such as a CD or DVD that is not included in the version you purchased, you may download this material at http://booksupport.wiley.com. For more information about Wiley products, visit www.wiley.com.

Library of Congress Control Number: 2016932284

About the Authors

Ilya Ganelin is a roboticist turned data engineer. After a few years at the University of Michigan building self-discovering robots and another few years working on embedded DSP software with cell phones and radios at Boeing, he landed in the world of Big Data at the Capital One Data Innovation Lab. Ilya is an active contributor to the core components of Apache Spark and a committer to Apache Apex, with the goal of learning what it takes to build a next-generation distributed computing platform. Ilya is an avid bread maker and cook, skier, and race-car driver.

Ema Orhian is a passionate Big Data Engineer interested in scaling algorithms. She is actively involved in the Big Data community, organizing and speaking at conferences, and contributing to open source projects. She is the main committer on jaws-spark-sql-rest, a data warehouse explorer on top of Spark SQL. Ema has been working on bringing Big Data analytics into healthcare, developing an end-to-end pipeline for computing statistical metrics on top of large datasets.

Kai Sasaki is a Japanese software engineer who is interested in distributed computing and machine learning. Although the beginning of his career didn't start with Hadoop or Spark, his original interest toward middleware and fundamental technologies that support a lot of these services and the Internet drives him toward this field. He has been a Spark contributor who develops mainly MLlib and ML libraries. Nowadays, he is trying to research the great potential of combining deep learning and Big Data. He believes that Spark can play a significant role even in artificial intelligence in the Big Data era. GitHub: `https://github.com/Lewuathe`.

Brennon York is an aerobatic pilot moonlighting as a computer scientist. His true loves are distributed computing, scalable architectures, and programming languages. He has been a core contributor to Apache Spark since 2014 with the goal of developing a stronger community and inspiring collaboration through development on GraphX and the core build environment. He has had a relationship with Spark since his contributions began and has been taking applications into production with the framework since that time.

About the Technical Editors

Ted Yu is a Staff Engineer at HortonWorks. He is also an HBase PMC and Spark contributor and has been using/contributing to Spark for more than one year.

Dan Osipov is a Principal Consultant at Applicative, LLC. He has been working with Spark for the last two years, and has been working in Scala for about four years, primarily with data tools and applications. Previously he was involved in mobile development and content management systems.

Jeff Thompson is a neuro-scientist turned data scientist with a PhD from UC Berkeley in vision science (primarily neuroscience and brain imaging), and a post-doc at Boston University's bio-medical imaging center. He has spent a few years working at a homeland security startup as an algorithms engineer building next-gen cargo screening systems. For the last two years he has been a senior data scientist at Bosch, a global engineering and manu-facturing company.

Anant Asthana is a Big Data consultant and Data Scientist at Pythian. He has a background in device drivers and high availability/critical load database systems.

Bernardo Palacio Gomez is a Consulting Member of the Technical Staff at Oracle on the Big Data Cloud Service Team.

Gaspar Munoz works for Stratio (`http://www.stratio.com`) as a product architect. Stratio was the first Big Data platform based on Spark, so he has worked with Spark since it was in the incubator. He has put into production several projects using Spark core, Streaming, and SQL for some of the most important banks in Spain. He has also contributed to Spark and the spark-csv projects.

Brian Gawalt received a Ph.D. in electrical engineering from UC Berkeley in 2012. Since then he has been working in Silicon Valley as a data scientist, specializing in machine learning over large datasets.

Adamos Loizou is a Java/Scala Developer at OVO Energy.

Credits

Project Editor
Charlotte Kughen

Production Editor
Christine O'Connor

Technical Editors
Ted Yu
Dan Osipov
Jeff Thompson
Anant Asthana
Bernardo Palacio Gomez
Gaspar Munoz
Brian Gawalt
Adamos Loizou

Production Manager
Kathleen Wisor

**Manager of Content Development
& Assembly**
Mary Beth Wakefield

Marketing Director
David Mayhew

Marketing Manager
Carrie Sherrill

**Professional Technology & Strategy
Director**
Barry Pruett

Business Manager
Amy Knies

Associate Publisher
Jim Minatel

Project Coordinator, Cover
Brent Savage

Proofreader
Nancy Carrasco

Indexer
John Sleeva

Cover Designer
Wiley

Cover Image
ktsimage/iStockphoto

Acknowledgments

We would like to offer a special thank you to Yuichi-Tanaka who worked with Kai to provide the use case example found in Chapter 6.

We would like to acknowledge and thank each of the authors for contributing their knowledge to make this book possible. Further we would like to thank the editors for their time and Wiley as our publisher.

The authors came from various companies and we want to thank the individual companies that were able to aid in the success of this book, even from a secondhand nature, in giving each of them the ability to write about their individual experiences they've had, both personally and in the field. With that, we would like to thank Capital One.

We would also like to thank the various other companies that are contributing in myriad ways to better Apache Spark as a whole. These include, but are certainly not limited to (and we apologize if we missed any), DataBricks, IBM, Cloudera, and TypeSafe.

Finally, this book would not have been possible without the ongoing work of the people who've contributed to the Apache Spark project, including the Spark Committers, the Spark Project Management Committee, and the Apache Software Foundation.

Contents at a glance

Contents

Introduction

Apache Spark is a distributed compute framework for easy, at-scale, computation. Some refer to it as a "compute grid" or a "compute framework"—these terms are also correct within the underlying premise that Spark makes it easy for developers to gain access and insight into vast quantities of data.

Apache Spark was created by Matei Zaharia as a research project inside of the University of California, Berkeley in 2009. It was donated to the open source community in 2010. In 2013 Spark was added into the Apache Software Foundation as an Incubator project and graduated into a Top Level Project (TLP) in 2014, where it remains today.

Who This Book Is For

If you've picked up this book we presume that you already have an extended fascination with Apache Spark. We consider the intended audience for this book to be one of a developer, a project lead for a Spark application, or a system administrator (or DevOps) who needs to prepare to take a developed Spark application into a migratory path for a production workflow.

What This Book Covers

This book covers various methodologies, components, and best practices for developing and maintaining a production-grade Spark application. That said, we presume that you already have an initial or possible application scoped for production as well as a known foundation for Spark basics.

How This Book Is Structured

This book is divided into six chapters, with the aim of imparting readers with the following knowledge:

- A deep understanding of the Spark internals as well as their implication on the production workflow
- A set of guidelines and trade-offs on the various configuration parameters that can be used to tune Spark for high availability and fault tolerance
- A complete picture of a production workflow and the various components necessary to migrate an application into a production workflow

What You Need to Use This Book

You should understand the basics of development and usage atop Apache Spark. This book *will not* be covering introductory material. There are numerous books, forums, and resources available that cover this topic and, as such, we assume all readers have basic Spark knowledge or, if duly lost, will read the interested topics to better understand the material presented in this book.

The source code for the samples is available for download from the Wiley website at: `www.wiley.com/go/sparkbigdataclustercomputing`.

Conventions

To help you get the most from the text and keep track of what's happening, we've used a number of conventions throughout the book.

> **NOTE** Notes indicate notes, tips, hints, tricks, or asides to the current discussion. As for styles in the text:
> - We *highlight* new terms and important words when we introduce them.
> - We show code within the text like so: `persistence.properties`.

Source Code

As you work through the examples in this book, you may choose either to type in all the code manually, or to use the source code files that accompany the book. All the source code used in this book is available for download at `www.wiley.com`.

Specifically for this book, the code download is on the Download Code tab at
www.wiley.com/go/sparkbigdataclustercomputing.

You can also search for the book at www.wiley.com by ISBN.

You can also find the files at https://github.com/backstopmedia/sparkbook.

NOTE   Because many books have similar titles, you may find it easiest to search by
ISBN; this book's ISBN is 978-1-119-25401-0.

Once you download the code, just decompress it with your favorite compression
tool.

Finishing Your Spark Job

When you scale out a Spark application for the first time, one of the more common occurrences you will encounter is the application's inability to merely succeed and finish its job. The Apache Spark framework's ability to scale is tremendous, but it does not come out of the box with those properties. Spark was created, first and foremost, to be a framework that would be easy to get started and use. Once you have developed an initial application, however, you will then need to take the additional exercise of gaining deeper knowledge of Spark's internals and configurations to take the job to the next stage.

In this chapter we lay the groundwork for getting a Spark application to succeed. We will focus primarily on the hardware and system-level design choices you need to set up and consider before you can work through the various Spark-specific issues to move an application into production.

We will begin by discussing the various ways you can install a production-grade cluster for Apache Spark. We will include the scaling efficiencies you will need depending on a given workload, the various installation methods, and the common setups. Next, we will take a look at the historical origins of Spark in order to better understand its design and to allow you to best judge when it is the right tool for your jobs. Following that, we will take a look at resource management: how memory, CPU, and disk usage come into play when creating and executing Spark applications. Next, we will cover storage capabilities within Spark and their external subsystems. Finally, we will conclude with a discussion of how to instrument and monitor a Spark application.

Installation of the Necessary Components

Before you can begin to migrate an application written in Apache Spark you will need an actual cluster to begin testing it on. You can download, compile, and install Spark in a number of different ways within its system (some will be easier than others), and we'll cover the primary methods in this chapter.

Let's begin by explaining how to configure a *native* installation, meaning one where *only* Apache Spark is installed, then we'll move into the various Hadoop distributions (Cloudera and Hortonworks), and conclude by providing a brief explanation on how to deploy Spark on Amazon Web Services (AWS).

Before diving too far into the various ways you can install Spark, the obvious question that arises is, "What type of hardware should I leverage for a Spark cluster?" We can offer various possible answers to this question, but we'd like to focus on a few resounding truths of the Spark framework rather than necessitating a given layout.

It's important to know that Apache Spark is an *in-memory* compute grid. Therefore, for maximum efficiency, it is highly recommended that the system, as a whole, maintain enough memory *within the framework* for the largest workload (or dataset) that will be conceivably consumed. We are not saying that you cannot scale a cluster later, but it is always better to plan ahead, especially if you work inside a larger organization where purchase orders might take weeks or months.

On the concept of memory it is necessary to understand that when computing the amount of memory you need to understand that the computation does not equate to a one-to-one fashion. That is to say, for a given 1TB dataset, you will need *more* than 1TB of memory. This is because when you create objects within Java from a dataset, the object is typically much larger than the original data element. Multiply that expansion times the number of objects created for a given dataset and you will have a much more accurate representation of the amount of memory a system will require to perform a given task.

To better attack this problem, Spark is, at the time of this writing, working on what Apache has called *Project Tungsten*, which will greatly reduce the memory overhead of objects by leveraging off heap memory. You don't need to know more about Tungsten as you continue reading this book, but this information may apply to future Spark releases, because Tungsten is poised to become the de facto memory management system.

The second major component we want to highlight in this chapter is the number of CPU cores you will need per physical machine when you are determining hardware for Apache Spark. This is a much more fragmented answer in that, once the data load normalizes into memory, the application is typically network or CPU bound. That said, the easiest solution is to test your Spark application on a smaller dataset and measure its bounding case, be it either network or CPU, and then plan accordingly from there.

Native Installation Using a Spark Standalone Cluster

The simplest way to install Spark is to deploy a Spark Standalone cluster. In this mode, you deploy a Spark binary to each node in a cluster, update a small set of configuration files, and then start the appropriate processes on the master and slave nodes. In Chapter 2, we discuss this process in detail and present a simple scenario covering installation, deployment, and execution of a basic Spark job.

Because Spark is not tied to the Hadoop ecosystem, this mode does not have any dependencies aside from the Java JDK. Spark currently recommends the Java 1.7 JDK. If you wish to run alongside an existing Hadoop deployment, you can launch the Spark processes on the same machines as the Hadoop installation and configure the Spark environment variables to include the Hadoop configuration.

> **NOTE** For more on a Cloudera installation of Spark try `http://www.cloudera .com/content/www/en-us/documentation/enterprise/latest/topics/ cdh_ig_spark_installation.html`. **For more on the Hortonworks installation try** `http://hortonworks.com/hadoop/spark/#section_6`. **And for more on an Amazon Web Services installation of Spark try** `http://aws.amazon.com/ articles/4926593393724923`.

The History of Distributed Computing That Led to Spark

We have introduced Spark as a distributed compute framework; however, we haven't really discussed what this means. Until recently, most computer systems available to both individuals and enterprises were based around single machines. These single machines came in many shapes and sizes and differed dramatically in terms of their performance, as they do today.

We're all familiar with the modern ecosystem of personal machines. At the low-end, we have tablets and mobile phones. We can think of these as relatively weak, un-networked computers. At the next level we have laptops and desktop computers. These are more powerful machines, with more storage and computational ability, and potentially, with one or more graphics cards (GPUs) that support certain types of massively parallel computations. Next are those machines that some people have networked with in their home, although generally these machines were not networked to share their computational ability, but rather to provide shared storage—for example, to share movies or music across a home network.

Within most enterprises, the picture today is still much the same. Although the machines used may be more powerful, most of the software they run, and most of the work they do, is still executed on a single machine. This fact limits the scale and the potential impact of the work they can do. Given this limitation, a few select organizations have driven the evolution of modern parallel computing to allow networked systems of computers to do more than just share data, and to collaboratively utilize their resources to tackle enormous problems.

In the public domain, you may have heard of the SETI at Home program from Berkeley or the Folding@Home program from Stanford. Both of these programs were early initiatives that let individuals dedicate their machines to solving parts of a massive distributed task. In the former case, SETI has been looking for unusual signals coming from outer space collected via radio telescope. In the latter, the Stanford program runs a piece of a program computing permutations of proteins—essentially building molecules—for medical research.

Because of the size of the data being processed, no single machine, not even the massive supercomputers available in certain universities or government agencies, have had the capacity to solve these problems within the scope of a project or even a lifetime. By distributing the workload to multiple machines, the problem became potentially tractable—solvable in the allotted time.

As these systems became more mature, and the computer science behind these systems was further developed, many organizations created *clusters* of machines—coordinated systems that could distribute the workload of a particular problem across many machines to extend the resources available. These systems first grew in research institutions and government agencies, but quickly moved into the public domain.

Enter the Cloud

The most well-known offering in this space is of course the proverbial "cloud." Amazon introduced AWS (Amazon Web Services), which was later followed by comparable offerings from Google, Microsoft, and others. The purpose of a cloud is to provide users and organizations with scalable clusters of machines that can be started and expanded upon on-demand.

At about the same time, universities and certain companies were also building their own clusters in-house and continuing to develop frameworks that focused on the challenging problem of parallelizing arbitrary types of tasks and computations. Google was born out of its PageRank algorithm—an extension of the MapReduce framework that allowed a general class of problems to be solved in parallel on clusters built with commodity hardware.

This notion of building algorithms, that, while not the most efficient, could be massively parallelized and scaled to thousands of machines, drove the next stage of growth in this area. The idea that you could solve massive problems by building clusters, not of supercomputers, but of relatively weak and inexpensive machines, democratized distributed computing.

Yahoo, in a bid to compete with Google, developed, and later open-sourced under the Apache Foundation, the Hadoop platform—an ecosystem for distributed computing that includes a file system (HDFS), a computation framework

(MapReduce), and a resource manager (YARN). Hadoop made it dramatically easier for any organization to not only create a cluster but to also create software and execute parallelizable programs on these clusters that can process huge amounts of distributed data on multiple machines.

Spark has subsequently evolved as a replacement for MapReduce by building on the idea of creating a framework to simplify the difficult task of writing parallelizable programs that efficiently solve problems at scale. Spark's primary contribution to this space is that it provides a powerful and simple API for performing complex, distributed operations on distributed data. Users can write Spark programs as if they were writing code for a single machine, but under the hood this work is distributed across a cluster. Secondly, Spark leverages the memory of a cluster to reduce MapReduce's dependency on the underlying distributed file system, leading to dramatic performance gains. By virtue of these improvements, Spark has achieved a substantial amount of success and popularity and has brought you here to learn more about how it accomplishes this.

Spark is not the right tool for every job. Because Spark is fundamentally designed around the MapReduce paradigm, its focus is on excelling at Extract, Transform, and Load (ETL) operations. This mode of processing is typically referred to as batch processing—processing large volumes of data efficiently in a distributed manner. The downside of batch processing is that it typically introduces larger latencies for any single piece of data. Although Spark developers have been dedicating a substantial amount of effort to improving the Spark Streaming mode, it remains fundamentally limited to computations on the order of seconds. Thus, for truly low-latency, high-throughput applications, Spark is not necessarily the right tool for the job. For a large set of use cases, Spark nonetheless excels at handling typical ETL workloads and provides substantial performance gains (as much as 100 times improvement) over traditional MapReduce.

Understanding Resource Management

In the chapter on cluster management you will learn more about how the operating system handles the allocation and distribution of resources amongst the processes on a single machine. However, in a distributed environment, the cluster manager handles this challenge. In general, we primarily focus on three types of resources within the Spark ecosystem. These are disk storage, CPU cores, and memory. Other resources exist, of course, such as more advanced abstractions like virtual memory, GPUs, and potentially different tiers of storage, but in general we don't need to focus on those within the context of building Spark applications.

Disk Storage

The first type of resource, disk, is vital to any Spark application since it stores persistent data, the results of intermediate computations, and system state.

When we refer to disk storage, we are referring to data stored on a hard drive of some kind, either the traditional rotating spindle, or newer SSDs and flash memory. Like any other resource, disk is finite. Disk storage is relatively cheap and most systems tend to have an abundance of physical storage, but in the world of big data, it's actually quite common to use up even this cheap and abundant storage! We tend to enable replication of data for the sake of durability and to support more efficient parallel computation. Also, you'll usually want to persist frequently used intermediate dataset(s) to disk to speed up long-running jobs. Thus, it generally pays to be cognizant of disk usage, and treat it as any other finite resource.

Interaction with physical disk storage on a single machine is abstracted away by the file system—a program that provides an API to read and write files. In a distributed environment, where data may be spread across multiple machines, but still needs to be accessed as a single logical entity, a *distributed* file system fulfills the same role. Managing the operation of the *distributed* file system and monitoring its state is typically the role of the cluster administrator, who tracks usage, quotas, and re-assigns resources as necessary. Cluster managers such as YARN or Mesos may also regulate access to the underlying file system to better distribute resources between simultaneously executing applications.

CPU Cores

The central processing unit (CPU) on a machine is the processor that actually executes all computations. Modern machines tend to have multiple CPU cores, meaning that they can execute multiple processes in parallel. In a cluster, we have multiple machines, each with multiple cores. On a single machine, the operating system handles communication and resource sharing between processes. In a distributed environment, the cluster manager handles the assignment of CPU resources (cores) to individual tasks and applications. In the chapter on cluster management, you'll learn specifically how YARN and Mesos ensure that multiple applications running in parallel can have access to this pool of available CPUs and share it fairly.

When building Spark applications, it's helpful to relate the number of CPU cores to the parallelism of your program, or how many tasks it can execute simultaneously. Spark is based around the resilient distributed dataset (RDD)—an abstraction that treats a distributed dataset as a single entity consisting of multiple partitions. In Spark, a single Spark task will processes a single partition of an RDD on a single CPU core.

Thus, the degree to which your data is partitioned—and the number of available cores—essentially dictates the parallelism of your program. If we consider a hypothetical Spark job consisting of five stages, each needing to run 500 tasks, if we only have five CPU cores available, this may take a long time to complete! In contrast, if we have 100 CPU cores available, and the data is sufficiently partitioned, for example into 200 partitions, Spark will be able to parallelize much more effectively, running 100 tasks simultaneously, completing the job much more quickly. By default, Spark only uses two cores with a single executor—thus when launching a Spark job for the first time, it may unexpectedly take a very long time. We discuss executor and core configuration in the next chapter.

Memory

Lastly, memory is absolutely critical to almost all Spark applications. Memory is used for internal Spark mechanisms such as the shuffle, and the JVM heap is used to persist RDDs in memory, minimizing disk I/O and providing dramatic performance gains. Spark acquires memory per executor—a worker abstraction that you'll learn more about in the next chapter. The amount of memory that Spark requests per executor is a configurable parameter and it is the job of the cluster manager to ensure that the requested resources are provided to the requesting application.

Generally, cluster managers assign memory the same way that the cluster manager assigns CPU cores as discrete resources. The total available memory in a cluster is broken up into blocks or containers, and these containers are assigned (or offered in the case of Mesos) to specific applications. In this way, the cluster manager can act to both assign memory fairly, and schedule resource usage to avoid starvation.

Each assigned block of memory in Spark is further subdivided based on Spark and cluster manager configurations. Spark makes tradeoffs between the memory allocated for dynamic memory allocated during shuffle, the memory used to store cached RDDs, and the amount of memory available for off-heap storage.

Most applications will require some degree of tuning to determine the appropriate balance of memory based on the RDD transformations executed within the Spark program. A Spark application with improperly configured memory settings may run inefficiently, for example, if RDDs cannot be fully persisted in memory and instead are swapped back and forth from disk. Insufficient memory allocated for the shuffle operation can also lead to slowdown since internal tables may be swapped to disk, if they cannot fit entirely into memory.

In the next chapter on cluster management, we will discuss in detail the memory structure of a block of memory allocated to Spark. Later, when we cover performance tuning, we'll show how to set the parameters associated with memory to ensure that Spark applications run efficiently and without failures.

In newer versions of Spark, starting with Spark 1.6, Spark introduces dynamic automatic memory tuning. As of 1.6, Spark will automatically adjust the fraction of memory allocated for shuffle and caching, as well as the total amount of allocated memory. This allows you to fit larger datasets into a smaller amount of memory, as well as to more easily create programs that execute successfully out of the box, without extensive tuning of a multitude of memory parameters.

Using Various Formats for Storage

When solving a distributed processing problem sometimes we get tempted to focus more on the solution, on how to get the best from the cluster resources, or on how to improve the code to be more efficient. All of these things are great but they are not all we can do to improve the performance of our application.

Sometimes, the way we choose to store the data we are processing, highly impacts the execution. This subchapter proposes to bring some light on how to decide which file format to choose when storing data.

There are several aspects we must consider when loading or storing data with Spark: What is the most suitable file format to choose? Is the file format splittable? Meaning, can splits of this file be processed in parallel? Do we compress the data and if so, which compression codec to use? How large should our files be?

The first thing you should be careful of is the file sizes your dataset is divided into. Even if in Chapter 3 you will read about parallelism and how it affects the performance of your application, it is important to mention how the file sizes determine the level of parallelism. As you already might know, on HDFS each file is stored in blocks. When reading these files with Spark, each HDFS block will be mapped to one Spark partition. For each partition, a Spark task will be launched to read and process it. A high level of parallelism is usually beneficial if you have the necessary resources and if the data is properly partitioned. However, a very large number of tasks come with a scheduling overhead that should be avoided if it is not necessary. In conclusion, the size of the files we are reading causes a proportional number of tasks to be launched and a significant scheduling overhead.

Besides the large number of tasks that are launched, reading a lot of small files also brings a serious time penalty inflicted by opening them. You should also consider the fact that all the file paths are handled on the driver. So if your data consists of a huge amount of small files, then you risk placing memory pressure on the driver.

 On the other hand, if the dataset is composed of a set of huge files, then you must make sure the files are splittable. Otherwise, they will have to be handled by single tasks resulting in very large partitions. This will highly decrease performance.

Most of the time, saving space is important. So, to minimize the data's disk footprint, we compress it. If we plan to process this data later on with Spark, we have to be careful which compression format we choose. It is important to know if it is splittable or not. Let's imagine we have a 5 GB file stored on HDFS with a block size of 128 MB. The file will be composed of 40 blocks. When we read it with Spark, a task will be launched for each block, so there will be 40 parallel tasks that will process the data. If this file would be a compressed file in gzip format, then it is not supported to decompress a block independently from the other blocks. This means that Spark is not able to process each block in parallel, so only one task will process the entire file. It is obvious that the performance is highly impacted and we might even face memory issues.

There are many compression codecs having different features and advantages. When choosing between them we trade off between compression ratio and speed. The most common ones are gzip, bzip2, lzo, lz4, and Snappy.

- Gzip is a compression codec that uses the DEFLATE algorithm. It is a wrapper around the Zlib compression format having the advantage of a good compression ratio.

- Bzip2 compression format uses the burrows wheeler transform algorithm and it is block oriented. This codec has a higher compression ratio than gzip.

- There are also the LZO and the LZ4 block oriented compression codecs that both are based on the LZ77 algorithm. They have modest compression ratios but they excel at compression and decompression speeds.

The fastest compression and decompression speed is provided by the Snappy compression codec. It is a block-oriented codec based on the LZ77 algorithm. Because of its decompression speed, it is desirable to use Snappy for datasets that are frequently used.

If we were to separate compression codecs into splittable or not splittable we would refer to Table 1-1. However, making this separation is confusing because it strongly depends on the file format that they are compressing. If the non splittable codecs are used with file formats that support block structure like Sequence files or ORC files, then the compression will be applied for each block. In this case, Spark will be able to launch in parallel tasks for each block. So you might consider them splittable. But, on the other hand, if they are used to compress text files, then the entire file will be compressed in a single block, therefore only one task will be launched per file.

This means that not only the compression codec is important but also the file's storage format. Spark supports a variety of input and output formats, structured or unstructured, starting with text files, sequence files, or any other Hadoop file formats. Is important to underline that making use of the `hadoopRDD` and `newHadoopRDD` methods, you can read in Spark any existent Hadoop file format.

Table 1-1: Splittable Compression Codecs

COMPRESSION CODEC	IS SPLITTABLE
Gzip	No
Bzip2	Yes
LZO	No, unless indexed
Snappy	Yes

Text Files

You can easily read text files with Spark using the `textFile` method. You can either read a single file or all of the files within a folder. Because this method will split the documents into lines, you have to keep the lines at a reasonable size.

As mentioned above, if the files are compressed, depending on the compression codec, they might not be splittable. In this case, they should have sizes small enough to be easily processed within a single task.

There are some special text file formats that must be mentioned: the structured text files. CSV files, JSON files and XML files all belong to this category.

To easily do some analytics over data stored in CSV format you should create a DataFrame on top of it. To do this you have two options: You can either read the files with the classic `textFile` method or programmatically specify the schema, or you could use one of the Databricks packages spark-csv. In the example below, we read a csv file, remove the first line that represents the header, and map each row to a Car object. The resulted RDD is transformed to a DataFrame.

```
import sqlContext.implicits._
case class Pet(name: String, race : String)
val textFileRdd = sc.textFile("file.csv")
val schemaLine = textFileRdd.first()
val noHeaderRdd = textFileRdd.filter(line => ⏎
!line.equals(schemaLine))
val petRdd = noHeaderRdd.map(textLine => {
          val columns = textLine.split(",")
          Pet(columns(0), columns(1))})
val petDF = petRdd.toDF()
```

An easier way to process CSV files is to use the spark-csv package from Databricks. You just read the file specifying the csv format:

```
val df = sqlContext.read
    .format("com.databricks.spark.csv")
    .option("header", "true")
    .option("inferSchema", "true")
    .load("file.csv")
```

To read and process JSON files, Spark SQL exposes a dedicated method. You have the possibility to leave Spark SQL to infer the schema from the dataset or you can specify it programmatically. If you know the schema in advance, it is recommended to provide it. This is to avoid making Spark go through the input once more to determine it. Another advantage of providing the schema yourself is that you have the possibility of working only with the fields you need. If you have JSON files with lots of fields that are not in your interest, you can specify only the relevant ones and the other ones will be ignored.

Here is an example of how to read a JSON file with and without specifying the schema of your dataset:

```
val schema = new StructType(Array(
    new StructField("name", StringType, false),
    new StructField("age", IntegerType, false)))
val specifiedSchema= sqlContext.jsonFile("file.json",schema)
val inferedSchema = sqlContext.jsonFile("file.json")
```

This way of handling JSON files assumes that you have a JSON object per line. If there are some JSON objects that miss several fields then the fields are replaced with nulls. In the case when we infer the schema and there are mal-formed inputs, Spark SQL creates a new column called _corrupt_record. The erroneous inputs will have this column populated with their data and will have all the other columns null.

The XML file formats are not an ideal format for distributed processing because they usually are very verbose and don't have an XML object per line. Because of this they cannot be processed in parallel. Spark doesn't have for now a built-in library for processing these files. If you try to read an XML file with the textFile method it is not useful because Spark will read the file line by line. If your XML files are small enough to fit in memory, then you could read them using the wholeTextFile method. This will output a pair RDD that will have the file's path as key and the entire text file as value. Processing large files in this manner is allowed but it might cause a bad performance.

Sequence Files

Sequence files are a commonly used file format, consisting of binary key value pairs that must be subclasses of the Hadoop Writable interface. They are very popular in distributed processing because they have sync markers. This allows you to identify record boundaries, thus making it possible to parallelize the process. Sequence files are an efficient way of storing your data because they can be efficiently processed compressed or uncompressed.

Spark offers a dedicated API for loading sequence files:

```
val seqRdd = sc.sequenceFile("filePath", classOf[Int], classOf[String])
```

Avro Files

The avro file format is a binary data format that relies on a schema. When storing data into an avro format, the schema is always stored with the data. This feature makes possible for files in avro file format to be read from different applications.

There is a Spark package to read/write avro files: spark-avro (`https://github`
`.com/databricks/spark-avro`). This package handles the schema conversion
from avro schema to the Spark SQL schema. To load an avro file is pretty straight
forward: You have to include the spark-avro package and then you read the file
as follows:

```
import com.databricks.spark.avro._
val avroDF = sqlContext.read.avro("pathToAvroFile")
```

Parquet Files

Parquet file format is a columnar file format that supports nested data
structures. Being in a columnar format makes it very good for aggregation
queries, because only the required columns are read from disk. Parquet
files support really efficient compression and encoding schemes, since they
can be specified per-column. This being said, it is clear why using this file
format gives you the advantage of decreasing the disk IO operations and
saving more storage space.

Spark SQL provides methods for reading and writing Parquet files
maintaining the data's schema. This file format supports schema evolution.
One can start with some columns and then add more columns. These
schema differences are automatically detected and merged. However if
you can, you should avoid schema merging, because it is an expensive
operation. Below is an example of how to read a parquet file, having the
schema merging enabled:

```
val parquetDF = sqlContext.read
                .option("mergeSchema","true")
                .parquet("parquetFolder")
```

In Spark SQL, the Parquet Datasource is able to detect if data is partitioned and to determine the partitions. This is an important optimization in data analysis because during a query, only the needed partitions
are scanned based on the predicates inside the query. In the example
below, only the folder for company A will be scanned in order to serve
the requested employees.

```
Folder/company=A/file1.parquet
Folder/company=B/fileX.parquet

SELECT employees FROM myTable WHERE company=A
```

The Parquet file format is encouraged as a best practice for Spark SQL.

Making Sense of Monitoring and Instrumentation

One of the most important things when running a distributing application is monitoring. You want to identify as soon as possible anomalies and to troubleshoot them. You want to analyze the application's behavior so you can determine how to improve its performance. Knowing how your application uses the cluster resources and how the load is distributed might make you gain some important insights and save you a lot of time and money.

The purpose of this section is to identify the monitoring options we have and what we learn from the metrics we inspect.

Spark UI

Spark comes with a built-in UI that exposes useful information and metrics about the application you are running. When you launch a Spark application, a web user interface is launched, having the default port set on 4040. If there are multiple Spark drivers running on the node, then an exception will be displayed reporting the fact that the 4040 port is unavailable. In this case, the web UI will try to bind to the next ports starting with 4040: 4041, 4042 until an available one is found.

To access the Spark UI for your application, you will open the following page in your web browser: `http://<driver-node-ip>:<allocatedPort-default4040>`.

The default behavior is to provide access to the job execution metrics only during the execution of your application. So, you will be able to see the Spark UI as long as the application is still running. To continue seeing this information in the UI even after the process finishes, you can change the default behavior by setting the `spark.eventLog.enabled` to true.

This feature is really useful, because you can understand better the behavior of your Spark application. In this web user interface you can see information such as:

- In the Jobs tab you can see the list of jobs that were executed and the job that is still in progress with their execution timeline. It displays how many stages and tasks were successful from the total number and information about the duration of each job (see Figure 1-1).

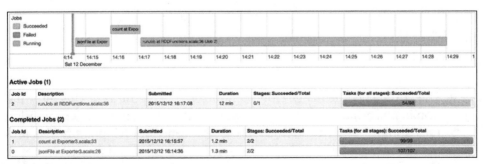

Figure 1-1: The Spark UI showing job progress

■ In the Stages tab you can see the list of stages that were executed and the one that is still active for all of the jobs (see Figure 1-2). This page offers relevant information about how your data is being processed: You can see the amount of data that is received as an input and its size as an output. Also, here you can see the amount of data that is being shuffled. This information is valuable since it might signal that you are not using the right operators for processing your data or that you might need to partition your data. In Chapter 3 there are more details about the shuffle phase and how it impacts the performance of your Spark application.

Active Stages (1)

Stage Id	Description				Submitted	Duration	Tasks: Succeeded/Total	Input	Output	Shuffle Read	Shuffle Write
4	runJob at RDDFunctions.scala:36	+details	(kill)		2015/12/13 01:07:33	4.4 min	1/113	656.9 MB	1710.2 MB		

Completed Stages (4)

Stage Id	Description		Submitted	Duration	Tasks: Succeeded/Total	Input	Output	Shuffle Read	Shuffle Write
3	count at Exporter3.scala:33	+details	2015/12/13 01:07:31	0.1 s	1/1			4.6 KB	
2	count at Exporter3.scala:33	+details	2015/12/13 01:06:15	1.3 min	113/113	14.0 GB			4.6 KB
1	jsonFile at Exporter3.scala:26	+details	2015/12/13 01:06:12	0.5 s	10/10			60.3 KB	
0	jsonFile at Exporter3.scala:26	+details	2015/12/13 01:04:52	1.3 min	113/113	8.7 GB			60.3 KB

Figure 1-2: Spark UI job execution information

■ In the task metrics stage, you can analyze metrics about the tasks that were executed. You can see reports about their duration, about garbage collection, memory, and the size of the data that is being processed (see Figure 1-3). The information about the duration of the running tasks might signal that your data is not uniformly distributed. If the maximum task duration is a lot larger than the medium duration it means that you have a task on which the load is much higher than on the others.

Summary Metrics for 96 Completed Tasks

Metric	Min	25th percentile	Median	75th percentile	Max
Duration	10 s	20 s	23 s	26 s	32 s
GC Time	0.3 s	2 s	2 s	2 s	2 s
Peak Execution Memory	4.3 MB	106.3 MB	208.3 MB	310.4 MB	408.2 MB
Input Size / Records	75.3 MB / 79837	128.1 MB / 133624	128.1 MB / 134679	128.1 MB / 136837	128.1 MB / 145307
Shuffle Write Size / Records	42.0 B / 1	42.0 B / 1	42.0 B / 1	42.0 B / 1	42.0 B / 1

Figure 1-3: Spark UI task metrics

■ The DAG schedules stages for a certain job (see Figure 1-4). This information is important for you to understand the way your job is scheduled for running. You can identify the operations that trigger shuffles and are stage boundaries. Chapter 3 goes into more detail about the Spark Execution Engine.

- Information about the execution environment: In the Environment tab you can see all the configuration parameters used when starting your Spark context and the JARs used.

- Logs gathered from each executor are also important.

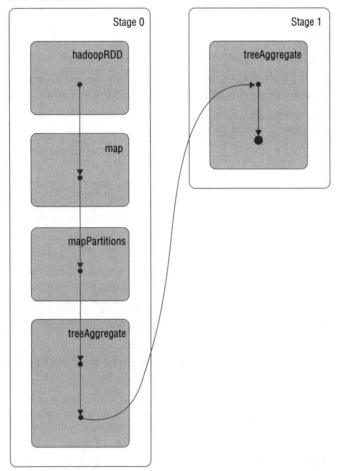

Figure 1-4: The DAG stage scheduling

Spark Standalone UI

When running Spark in standalone mode, you have another build in the web user interface that exposes information about clusters and about the executed jobs and detailed logs. You can access this UI at the following address: `http://<master-ip>:<defaultPort: 8080>`.

If you are running Spark on top of YARN or Mesos cluster managers, you can start a history server that allows you to see the UI for applications that finished executing. To start the server use the following command: `./sbin/start-history-server.sh`.

The history server is available at the following address: `http://<server-url>:18080`.

Metrics REST API

Spark also provides REST APIs for retrieving metrics about your application for you to use programmatically or to build your own visualizations based on them. The information is provided in JSON format for running applications and for apps from history.

The API endpoints are :

```
http://<server-url>:18080/api/v1
http://<driver-node-ip>:<allocatedPort-default4040>
/api/v1
```

You can find more information about the available APIs at `http://spark.apache.org/docs/latest/monitoring.html#rest-api`.

Metrics System

A useful Spark component is the Metrics System. This system is available on the driver and on each executor and can expose information about several Spark components to different syncs. In this way you can obtain metrics sent by the master process, by your application, by worker processes, and by the driver and executors.

Spark offers the freedom to monitor your application using a different set of third-party tools using this Metrics System.

External Monitoring Tools

There are several external Spark monitoring applications used for profiling. A widely used open source tool for displaying time series data is Graphite. The Spark Metrics System has a built-in Graphite sink that sends metrics about your application to a Graphite node.

You could also use Ganglia, a scalable distributed monitoring system to keep an eye on your application. Among other metrics' syncs, Spark supports a Ganglia sync that sends the metrics to a Ganglia node or to a multicast group. Because of licensing reasons this sync is not included in the default Spark build.

Another performance monitoring tool for Spark is SPM. This tool collects all the metrics from your Spark application and provides monitoring charts.

Summary

In this chapter we detailed the ways that you can install a production-grade cluster for Apache Spark. We also covered a bit about scaling efficiencies, along with installation and setup. You should now have a good idea about how Spark handles resource management and its various storage capabilities and external subsystems. And, we showed you how to instrument and monitor a Spark application. Now, in Chapter 2 you will learn all about cluster management, Spark's physical processes and how they are managed by components inside the Spark engine.

Cluster Management

In Chapter 1, we learned about some of the history of distributed computing, and how Spark developed within the broader data ecosystem. Much of the challenge of working with distributed systems simply comes from managing the resources that these systems need in order to run. The fundamental problem is one of scarcity—there are a finite number of sparse resources, and a multitude of applications that demand these resources to execute. Distributed computing would not be possible without a system managing these resources and scheduling their distribution.

The power of Spark is that it abstracts away much of the heavy lifting of creating parallelized applications that can easily migrate from running on a single machine to running in a distributed environment. Cluster management tools play a critical role in this abstraction. The cluster manager abstracts away the complex dance of resource scheduling and distribution from the application, in our case—Spark. This makes it possible for Spark to readily make use of the resources of one machine, ten machines, or a thousand machines, without fundamentally changing its underlying implementation.

Spark is built on layers of abstractions that ultimately resolve into a simple and intuitive interface for its users. The core abstraction of the *RDD*, or *DataFrame*, transforms what would otherwise be a multitude of data stored in a distributed environment, into a single object that masks the distributed nature of the data. Under the hood, Spark handles the movement of data back and forth between machines so the user never has to manually organize their data. Because of this, it's much easier to reason logically about the applications you're writing, allowing you to easily create complex applications. You can focus on broadly scoped tasks and write declarative language to solve problems instead of worrying about and managing the internals of the system.

Spark users can focus on the more valuable task of combining data in meaningful ways to extract insights and meaning. This is because users don't have to worry about the underlying organization of data, how to aggregate data in the right place for the right piece of computation, or how data is physically distributed within the cluster. This approach lets the Spark engine handle the complicated process of translating logical operational flows into distributed physical processes and allows you (the user) to focus on creating functional applications.

In this chapter, you'll first learn about these physical processes, and how these physical processes are managed by components inside the Spark engine. These individual components are deployed in different ways in distributed environments. How they interact remains consistent, but the physical environment in which these Spark components actually execute is what changes. We will learn about the existing tools for cluster management that are responsible for coordinating the behavior of these components and look at specific execution scenarios.

The three cluster management tools that we consider here—Spark Standalone, YARN, and Mesos, approach the challenge of resource management in fundamentally different ways. This makes each better at certain things, and weaker in other areas. The goal of this chapter is for you to understand the strengths and weaknesses of each of these frameworks, how to use them, and which framework is ultimately the correct choice for your use case.

To provide a deeper understanding of how each of these tools work, we will also take a brief look at how an operating system manages resources on a single machine, and then generalize this to the broader use case of managing resources in a distributed environment. Lastly, we will develop a concrete understanding of Spark's resource model—how it manages memory and compute resources, and look at those Spark configurations that relate to resource management.

At first glance it may seem strange to dive deep into the low-level architecture powering Spark, given that it's designed specifically to provide high-level abstractions that hide these mechanisms. However, the key takeaway of all this is that by understanding the lower-level architecture, you can write programs to explicitly take advantage of this knowledge and work symbiotically with the physical execution environment. Spark is not yet a perfectly engineered system—by understanding these internals, you will be better able to identify the root causes of application failures, even given Spark's sometimes cryptic messages. Moreover, you will understand not just how to get your applications to complete, but how to optimize them to be good cluster citizens and good tenants of the broader ecosystem.

Background

The purpose of a cluster manager is to allocate physical resources that can actually execute logical code. In many ways, a cluster manager is a generalization of an operating system on a single machine, and it must deal with many of the same challenges. To motivate the need for a cluster management tool, it's helpful to understand the core concepts of an operating system since these same concepts are ultimately implemented in a variety of ways within the distributed ecosystem.

On a single machine, the role of the operating system (OS) is to define an interface between the physical hardware of the machine and the software that runs on top of it (see Figure 2-1). This involves a multitude of challenges including defining the language of communication, the scheduling of tasks and processes, and the allocation of resources to these processes. Modern operating systems create an abstraction—a simplified interface that hides the underlying complexity between the user of the operating system and the hardware that ultimately runs the software.

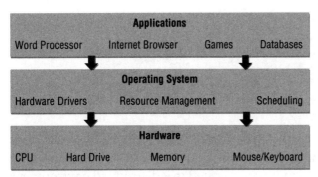

Figure 2-1: Operating system abstractions

Because of this abstraction, users of the operating system do not need to understand explicitly how to acquire resources for the programs that they want to run. In modern systems where many applications run simultaneously, users also do not need to worry about how to share resources between these applications. Users don't need to explicitly define the order in which applications execute nor how they should access resources at the same time. Ultimately, all the user cares about is that the application they submit runs to completion and produces an accurate result.

Under the hood, the operating system handles the delicate dance of scheduling and resource management. A process running inside the OS requires memory to store data it needs to execute, it needs access to the hard drive to retrieve and write data that's too large to fit into memory, and it needs access to the CPU to actually perform its operations. To ensure that all processes are able to run, the OS will run a scheduler that ensures that each process gets a fair share of CPU execution time.

To allow processes to have the data they need, the OS handles the task of assigning unique blocks of memory to each process and it provides the interface to each process that allows it to read from and write data to disk. The lower-level interfaces that define how the OS controls the physical devices is hidden from the individual programs requesting the resource. Again, these programs simply need to know how to get resources when they need them. Figure 2-2 shows a high-level view of how resources in an operating system are shared between processes.

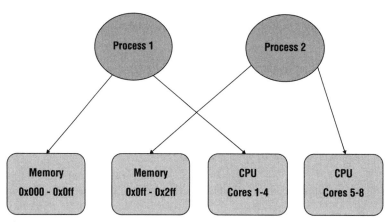

Figure 2-2: Process execution in an OS

The OS takes care of all these tasks and more. This process is no mean feat on a single machine, and it's even more complicated in a distributed environment. In a distributed environment, we deal with several additional challenges. The first of these is scalability—when adding hardware resources, especially in a network, we introduce complexity to the system. We potentially introduce lag time between components, and we add the overhead of network communication.

We also deal with the added challenge of durability—all hardware has an expected rate of failure, and while the likelihood of any individual piece failing is low, the more hardware you have in a system, the higher the likelihood that a component will fail at some point in time. On a single machine, it's highly unlikely for components to no longer be able to talk to each other—for example the messaging bus between the main memory and the CPU on a computer motherboard is a highly reliable component.

However, in a distributed environment—a system of networked computers typically referred to as a cluster—network failures can and do happen, so different machines may no longer be able to communicate with each other. Thus, distributed systems have to deal with the additional challenge of being resilient to failures both on any single machine, and on failures between machines. An even harder problem to detect and resolve is when a node is operating, but with degraded performance.

A system remaining operational in all scenarios is referred to as availability, and this requirement, particularly in production environments, is oftentimes a major sticking point. A system that remains operational even given failures of individual components without interruption of service is called a highly available system. The desire for systems that do not fail catastrophically, and the accompanying need for dynamic addition and loss of resources, is what has driven the design of most modern cluster management tools.

Managing resources in a distributed environment is thus a complex challenge, especially when many concurrent users share this environment. When many users share the same environment, they may make conflicting requests to the system. For example, two users may both request 70% of the available memory of a system at the same time, which is something that is clearly physically impossible. A cluster manager can deal with this conflict by explicitly scheduling when the users get specific resources or by negotiating with the requesting user or application.

The cluster manager ensures that all applications have the resources they need by coordinating the allocation and recovery of resources to processes executing in the cluster. It is thus a direct analog to the operating system with the added complexity of there being a physical separation between the centralized cluster manager and the hardware resources that it ultimately manages.

In general, the cluster manager will not supplant the operating system on any individual machine. Instead, the cluster manager emulates an operating system across multiple machines, and on any individual machine, leverages the local operating system for the more fine-grained control of local resources and access to the physical hardware. The cluster manager therefore primarily deals with the more general task of fair resource scheduling.

In the same manner that an OS on a single machine ensures that multiple processes can run simultaneously with the resources they need, the cluster manger ensures that multiple applications running in a cluster can, at best, run simultaneously, or, at worst, that all applications will have the resources they need to complete. There are different approaches to the task of ensuring that each application has the memory, CPU, disk, and network resources that it needs and we will present a detailed discussion of how a few specific cluster managers accomplish this.

In this chapter, we will look at how Spark, as an example application using a cluster manager, acquires and leverages the resources that it needs to run a Spark job. As you'll learn later, when a Spark job is executed, Spark creates many simultaneous physical processes, each of which requires memory and CPU to execute. The cluster manager is responsible for dynamically allocating these resource chunks to these processes, and once complete, it makes these resources available for subsequent operations.

Currently, there are three ways to create a Spark cluster that can run distributed Spark operations, thus translating Spark's logical plan into code that runs simultaneously on multiple machines. The first option is to use the cluster manager packaged with Spark to create a Spark Standalone cluster. As an alternative, when running in a Hadoop environment you may use the YARN resource manager. Lastly, Spark also supports Mesos, a general framework for distributed resource management. For each of these frameworks we will discuss their architecture and the Spark setup and configuration. We will also look at a real-world deployment scenario and walk through the process of running an application in Spark standalone, Mesos, or YARN. For Mesos and YARN, we'll also learn about their support for dynamic resource allocation, allowing more efficient utilization of cluster resources.

Spark Components

Now that we understand the need for a cluster manager, let's next take a look at the main components of Spark since these are the components that ultimately execute via the cluster management tool (see Figure 2-3). There are a number of entities in the Spark ecosystem that collaborate to run your application. At a high level, everything begins with the driver. The driver is essentially an overseer that maintains connections to the other entities in the cluster and submits tasks for execution by the worker nodes in the cluster. Workers, in turn, run executor processes, which have one or more tasks, actually executing the code that makes up a Spark job. These entities are agnostic of the cluster manager, whether it's the Spark Master (in Spark Standalone), YARN, or Mesos. In this section we will look at these pieces in detail and learn how they interact.

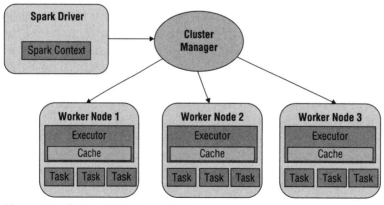

Figure 2-3: The Spark cluster architecture

Driver

The driver is the process responsible for launching and managing running Spark applications. Specifically, the driver is the entity that maintains connections to all the worker nodes, and translates the logical Spark application code into physical commands that are executed somewhere in the cluster. As the master process, the driver fulfills a number of responsibilities.

First and foremost, the driver maintains the Spark context—a program state that allows it to assign tasks to executors, as well as maintaining certain internal constructs, such as accumulators and broadcast variables. This context is what tracks application settings, as well as available resources.

Next, the driver handles communication with the cluster manager to request resources to execute the Spark application. Once these resources are available, the driver then creates an execution plan based on the logical code of the Spark application that it submits to the allocated worker nodes. The execution plan itself is a Directed Acyclical Graph (DAG) of actions and transformations. Spark optimizes this DAG to minimize the movement of data, and then an internal construct known as the DAG Scheduler actually breaks this DAG down further into individual stages and then tasks. A stage is a set of transformations that must be applied to the data contained in an RDD (see Figure 2-4).

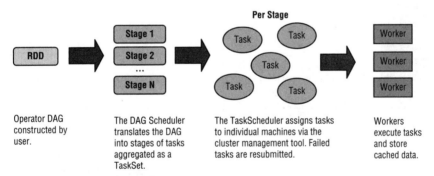

Figure 2-4: The Spark workflow

Data in Spark is broken up into *partitions*, meaning that while there is a single cohesive dataset, Spark does not operate on the entire dataset at once. Instead, this data is broken up into smaller pieces, each of which is operated on individually, allowing for increased parallelization. When the DAG scheduler subdivides a stage into tasks, it creates a new task for every partition of an RDD, such that each individual task is performing the same operation, but on a different piece of the data. The result of each individual task is later unified into a single RDD.

The DAG Scheduler handles the sub-division of the DAG into tasks and then another entity, the Task Scheduler, handles the scheduling of these tasks in the cluster. The Task Scheduler is aware of resource and locality constraints and assigns tasks to executors accordingly. Once the Task Scheduler has decided where the tasks should execute, the full DAG of transformations is serialized, along with the transformation closure—the data within the scope of the transformation—and transmitted over the network to a worker node where the appropriate executor then actually performs the necessary operations. The task Scheduler is also responsible for restarting failed or straggling tasks.

Workers and Executors

In a Spark cluster, the worker nodes are the physical machines that run executors and tasks. As a user, you never explicitly interact with the worker nodes, but under the hood the cluster manager communicates with the individual workers and handles resource allocation. Each worker has a fixed set of resources available to it, and these resources are explicitly allocated to the cluster manager. Because worker nodes may run multiple applications (not just Spark), limiting the resources available to the cluster manager allows for multi-tenancy and concurrent execution of different programs (see Figure 2-5).

1. Each worker runs one or more executor processes.

2. Each executor encapsulates CPU, memory, and disk access.

3. Each executor creates task threads and holds the RDD abstraction in memory to access its local data.

Figure 2-5: The worker architecture

Each worker node in a Spark cluster may run one more Spark executors—executors are an abstraction that allows for the configurable execution of a Spark program. Each executor runs a single Java Virtual Machine (JVM) and thus itself has a fixed set of resources. The number of resources, such as memory and CPU cores, allocated to the executor, as well as the number of overall executors, is a tunable parameter within Spark, and has a significant impact on the execution of an application.

Spark can only parallelize as much as its configuration allows. For example, if you have only allocated one executor and two cores for that executor, Spark can only run two processes in parallel since a single core runs a single process at a time. Moreover, for any individual operation, the amount of memory you have available is limited to the memory available to that one executor divided by the number of processes running within that executor.

Thus if you allocate 8GB of memory per executor and 8 CPU cores per executor, then each individual transformation has at most 1GB of memory available to it. The impact of this is that if these settings are improperly configured, and the underlying dataset is not partitioned into sufficiently small chunks of data, Spark may run out of memory when it operates on this data. This either causes memory errors or impacts performance as data is transferred back and forth from disk into memory.

When operationalizing a system, figuring out the right configuration balance is a key step, since you must consider the available resources of the system, as well as cluster manager configurations. Furthermore, you must understand how the executor interacts with other components of the system. For example, consider these two configurations:

```
--num-executors 5, --executor-cores 10
--num-executors 10, --executor-cores 5
```

When reading from HDFS it turns out that the second setting may perform better due to the way data is consumed from HDFS. The number of simultaneous operations that HDFS can support is a function of the number of HDFS blocks stored on the data node. Since the data being processed is split up across multiple nodes, depending on the size of your data and how it is distributed, you may achieve better performance by increasing the number of executors, rather than trying to have a large number of cores trying to read the same small fraction of the data on a single node.

As a computational framework, Spark necessarily defines a structure for the memory that it allocates. Within an operating system, for example, there is a subdivision in memory between the stack and the heap. The stack is the memory pool used to track program state, statically allocated memory, and local context. The heap is a memory pool used to dynamically allocate memory for new objects.

In Spark, because Spark provides the ability to leverage the memory available to it to cache data, it likewise subdivides the total memory available to any individual executor. Spark allows the user to explicitly configure the structure of this memory pool. When we look at configuration in the next section we'll talk about this parameterization in depth.

A single executor may have multiple tasks sharing this structured memory pool. Having multiple tasks within a single allocated block of resources reduces the overhead of certain Spark operations. For example, broadcast variables, which are a mechanism within Spark to support global data sharing, are replicated once per executor, not once per task. Having many more executors, each with fewer cores, can lead to unnecessary duplication of data.

Configuration

Some common parameters you would typically set are listed below. For a full list of available configurations and their effects, please refer to the Spark Configuration Guide (http://spark.apache.org/docs/latest/configuration.html).

The following settings are used on the command line when launching a new spark-shell or running the spark-submit script.

- `--num-executors N` — N is the number of executors to start across the cluster.

- `--executor-cores N` — N is the number of cores to run per executor, which is the number of concurrent tasks that a single executor may run. Recall that each core of the executor shares the total memory available to the executor.

- `--driver-memory Ng` — N is the number of gigabytes of memory to allocate for use by the driver. Driver memory is used to store accumulator variables as well as any outputs of the `collect()` operation. By default, the driver is allocated 1GB of memory in yarn-client mode and one core. If the application demands, it sometimes makes sense to increase this available memory, particularly for long-running Spark jobs, which may accumulate data during their execution. Here is an example:

```
spark-shell --num-executors 8 --executor-cores 5 --driver-memory 2g
```

Next, other settings are set within the Spark context, and provided either as a configuration file or set within the code itself. There are a few frequently used settings:

- `spark.executor.memory` — The amount of memory available to each executor (shared by all the cores).

- `spark.executor.extraJavaOptions` — JVM specific options that apply to each executor. This can be used to configure things like garbage collection and available heap memory.

- `spark.default.parallelis` — The default number of data partitions that Spark will use for computations.

Although we define the total memory allocated for an executor, how this memory is used is non-obvious. Spark needs different memory pools for different internal functions. There are two main subdivisions, on-heap and off-heap memory. Within the heap managed by the JVM, Spark makes tradeoffs between three separate pools of memory. How this memory is subdivided is shown in detail in Figure 2-6.

The first of these is the memory available to Spark to store persisted RDDs in Memory. A persisted RDD is an RDD that has been pinned in memory by calling the `cache()` or `persist()` functions, which, depending on the parameterization of that function, may store some that RDD in memory. Persisting the RDD in memory, rather than writing it to and reading it from disk every time, provides a dramatic performance boost, but because the amount of memory available is generally less than the amount of data being processed, you want to remain cognizant of which RDDs are pinned to memory. Spark supports configuration of different schemes for persisting this data in memory, allowing spillover to disk, for example. Within this first pool of memory there is something called the *unroll* memory, memory used during the conversion of serialized data to un-serialized data that can be operated on.

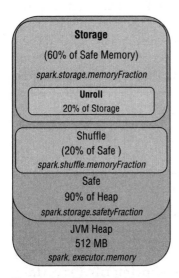

Figure 2-6: The Spark Memory structure

The second pool of memory that Spark defines is for the shuffle operation. The shuffle operation is a process by which Spark reorganizes the data being operated on for certain RDD transformations. For example, a `groupBy()` or `reduceByKey()` operation ultimately requires that all values associated with a particular key reside on the same node so that they can be aggregated within a single pool of memory. To accomplish this, Spark performs a shuffle—an all-all operation that moves all data between all nodes (for a single RDD) to co-locate data that requires it.

The shuffle is not a simple procedure—it requires serialization (the translation of Java in-memory objects into a byte stream), the transmission of this data over the network, and the overhead of additional memory to organize this data. Under the hood, Spark generates a number of lookup tables in memory, as well as buffering certain parts of the data in-flight for the sake of organization. Spark therefore exposes the configuration parameters for the shuffle operation, allowing you to tune its performance.

Because so much happens during the shuffle, it's a frequent point of failure and problems that are difficult to debug. Tuning shuffle parameters is often particularly valuable when optimizing programs for performance and stability. In Chapter 3, we look at the shuffle operation in detail and discuss how to tune it, and its memory usage, to ensure stability.

The final pool of memory is not explicitly defined, but is rather the memory remaining from the memory allocated to the executor after allocating memory for the shuffle, and for in-memory storage. The remaining space is unused and is left by Spark as overhead to avoid out of memory errors.

Off of the JVM heap, there is additional memory used to store certain special Java constructs that do not go on the heap. When we look at YARN and Mesos, we will introduce an additional parameter that allows the user to configure this. The JVM supports storing particular types of data off-heap, meaning that they are not subject to garbage collection. In newer versions of Spark, this off-heap memory is used to optimize Spark's performance but that is outside the scope of this discussion.

Thus, we have two parameters available to typically tune these three pools of memory (in addition to the `spark.executor.memory` parameter that defines the total amount of memory available):

- `spark.storage.memoryFraction`—This defines the fraction (by default 0.6) of the total memory to use for storing persisted RDDs.

- `spark.shuffle.memoryFraction`—This defines the fraction of memory to reserve for shuffle (by default 0.2).

You don't typically adjust the `spark.storage.unrollFraction` or the `spark.storage.safetyFraction`. These are defined primarily for certain internal constructs and size-estimation. These default to 20% and 90% respectively.

There are a multitude of other commonly used settings, but these are the ones most relevant to cluster deployment and configuration. Now that we understand the components at play within Spark, let's take a look at specific cluster management tools and learn what distinguishes them and how to get them up and running.

Spark Standalone

The first option available for cluster management is to use the cluster manager packaged with Spark. With Spark Standalone, one explicitly configures a master node and slaved workers. Then, there are a number of scripts that allow you to connect the master and the slaves. To install Spark Standalone to a cluster, one must manually deploy a compiled version of Spark to each node in your cluster. On each node in your cluster, you then set the appropriate configurations and environmental variables and then finally start all the masters and slaves.

In this section, we'll look briefly at the architecture of a Spark Standalone cluster and then walk through the setup of a Spark Standalone cluster.

Architecture

Spark Standalone is a very simple cluster manager. The machine where the Spark application is launched and where the Spark Context exists is the driver. In addition to the driver, with Spark Standalone there is also a master node, which fulfills the role of the cluster manager as we discussed in a previous section. The master node handles communication between the driver and the worker nodes and handles resource management. Lastly, we have a number of worker instances. There is no explicit requirement for the driver, master, and workers to be on separate machines. In fact, it's possible to start a Spark cluster on a single machine with multiple workers.

Single-Node Setup Scenario

First, we will walk through a simple scenario of setting up and configuring Spark on a single machine. This has the advantage of getting you up and running quickly, but will obviously provide you with a limited set of computational resources. While it's possible to configure everything using the command line, it will be easier to iterate and make subsequent changes if all configurations are specified in a file. Thus, we begin by creating a couple of configuration files inside the parent Spark directory.

First, we need to provide the location of the master and slave nodes. We do this by editing the template provided at `$SPARK_HOME/conf/slaves.template` and creating `$SPARK_HOME/conf/slaves`. Because we're running a local cluster, we can leave the default configuration of `localhost`.

Next, we can configure environment variables based on the template provided in `$SPARK_HOME/conf/spark-env.sh.template` and create `$SPARK_HOME/conf/spark-env.sh`. To configure a cluster, we need to set the following properties:

- First, set the memory available to each worker and the default setting for each executor—the latter can subsequently be configured as we discussed earlier.

  ```
  export SPARK_WORKER_MEMORY=2g
  export SPARK_EXECUTOR_MEMORY=512m
  ```

- Then, set the working directory for each worker where temporary files and logs can be stored.

  ```
  export SPARK_WORKER_DIR=/tmp/spark/data
  ```

- Once everything is configured, all that's left is to start the cluster by running:

  ```
  $SPARK_HOME/sbin/start-all.s
  ```

▪ And stop it with:

```
$SPARK_HOME/sbin/stop-all.sh
```

When running, you can open the Spark Standalone UI at `http://localhost:8080` and see the status of the cluster (see Figure 2-7).

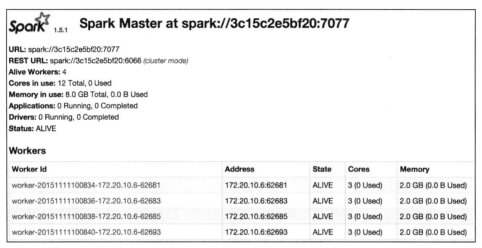

Figure 2-7: The Spark Standalone UI view

You can launch a Spark shell or submit a job (port 7077 is the default for master):

```
$SPARK_HOME/bin/spark-shell --master spark://$HOSTNAME:7077 ↵
--num-executors 4 --executor-cores 3
$SPARK_HOME/bin/spark-submit --master spark://$HOSTNAME:7077 ↵
--num-executors 4 --executor-cores 3 --class Main.class MyJar.jar
```

Multi-Node Setup

When creating workers on different machines, you have to edit your configurations and launch the workers slightly differently. First, for every host in the cluster, you must set:

```
export STANDALONE_SPARK_MASTER_HOST=$HOSTNAME
```

In the `$SPARK_HOME/conf/slaves` add an IP address for every machine in the cluster. For example:

```
192.168.1.50
192.168.1.51
192.168.1.52
```

To start the cluster automatically with `$SPARK_HOME/sbin/start-all.sh` you must either have pass-wordless SSH enabled between the machines in your cluster, or you can set the SPARK_SSH_FOREGROUND variable in spark-env .sh to be prompted for a password when connecting to remote hosts. Alternately, you can start the cluster manually by running:

```
$SPARK_HOME/sbin/start-master.sh on the master node and
$SPARK_HOME/sbin/start-slave.sh <master-URL> on each slave node
```

The Spark Standalone documentation discusses additional configuration options that are available.

YARN

Next, we'll look at running Spark on YARN. YARN is the cluster manager for Hadoop available as of Hadoop version 2.0. YARN evolved out of a need to provide a more scalable resource framework for MapReduce and as such has always been closely tied to the Hadoop ecosystem. Recently, YARN has moved toward becoming a more general resource scheduler, but it's not yet a standalone component. Thus, the following section applies only to running Spark within a Hadoop environment. Mesos, which we will look at in the next section, provides a general-purpose resource manager not tied to the Hadoop ecosystem.

Moving to a cluster manager such as YARN or Mesos provides a substantial benefit to anyone maintaining a cluster that runs a heterogeneous set of applications. The primary advantage of Spark Standalone is that it's very easy to configure and makes it possible to get up and running quickly with a minimum of effort. However, its primary limitation is that it provides no utility for sharing the physical resources of a cluster with non-Spark applications. If you have a scenario where you may have multiple groups sharing a cluster—some running Hive, some using HBase or Impala, and others running Spark, then you really need a cluster manager that can dynamically distribute resources between these different applications (see Figure 2-8). Otherwise, the task of managing resource allocation between these different applications becomes extremely cumbersome and complex.

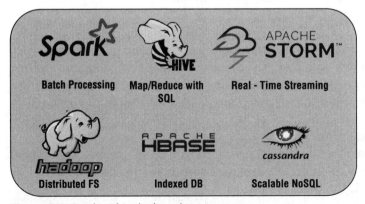

Figure 2-8: Spark within the broader ecosystem

While there are obvious advantages to running dedicated clusters, it's rare for a single tool to offer all the functionality necessary. For example, while Spark excels at batch processing, its support for indexing data or doing efficient lookups and search is limited. In contrast, HBase and Impala excel in this arena and having these running alongside Spark substantially expands the problem-set that a cluster is capable of handling. Spark's support for real-time stream processing is limited to processing on the order of seconds, while true streaming frameworks like Apache Storm can support millisecond-level latency. Although a dedicated cluster provides a level of simplicity and for any single application, can ensure that it has the optimal set of resources available to it, it can't support a wide variety of use cases, nor ensure fair resource sharing between applications.

Another advantage of running Spark on YARN (see Figure 2-9) is that it does not require any additional configuration or deployment of Spark binaries. When submitting a YARN application, one simply submits a compiled binary and YARN handles the distribution of that binary within the cluster. What this means is that for larger clusters, the sys-admin or dev-ops engineer can configure the cluster just once to use YARN, and then run a variety of applications without reconfiguring individual machines. Configuring individual worker nodes is unnecessary and deployment becomes much more straightforward.

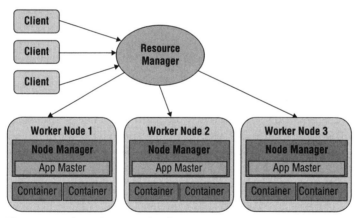

Figure 2-9: The YARN general architecture

Because YARN is usually found on most Hadoop clusters these days, it's also much simpler to migrate Spark workloads between clusters without needing to reinstall and reconfigure Spark on every new cluster. Thus, operationalizing a system based on Spark becomes a much more straightforward manner, which is why many companies run Spark either on top of YARN or on top of Mesos, instead of creating dedicated clusters.

In this section we'll look at the general architecture of a Spark deployment on top of YARN, how to configure dynamic resource allocation with YARN, and lastly look at a deployment scenario.

Architecture

Let's begin by looking at the architecture of YARN and how YARN fits into the Hadoop ecosystem. To YARN, Spark is just another application; thus when we discuss YARN's approach to resource allocation, all the concepts apply directly to the way that Spark executes on YARN.

Within YARN, there are two primary entities: the ResourceManager (RM) and the ApplicationMaster (AM). There is a third component: the NodeManager (NM), which is a slave of the ResourceManager. Broadly speaking, the ResourceManager controls a global pool of resources available within a cluster, subject to certain configurations and constraints. ZooKeeper, a cluster management tool widely used in distributed systems and in Hadoop, manages configuration and distributed services between Nodes.

For every application in the cluster, there is a framework-specific ApplicationMaster, for example, MapReduce and Spark would have their own versions of the ApplicationMaster. The ApplicationMaster requests resources from the ResourceManager, which then allocates them according to availability. The ApplicationMaster then coordinates with the NodeManager to execute individual tasks.

YARN's approach to resource allocation is to define a fundamental abstraction known as a *container*. A container is simply a set of resources—memory, CPU, network, disk, that are discretized as a finite set of resources available to the process running within that container. The ResourceManager has a utility called the Scheduler, which handles the allocation of containers to individual processes. The role of the Scheduler is both to assign the amount of resources, as well as to declare *when* a particular resource is available.

A typical workflow goes as follows: the Application Master requests a resource container from the ResourceManager and the NodeManager launches and monitors one or more of these containers on each individual Node. An application may request more resources than are available in a single container and the Application Master would consequently request multiple containers to fit this demand. YARN does not negotiate with the requesting application, so if the request cannot be fulfilled at the time it is made, YARN will block, and the requesting entity will be forced to wait until the resources become available.

When running a Spark application on YARN, the Spark application plugs transparently into the YARN ecosystem. With YARN, there is no notion of a worker as far as Spark is concerned. YARN is still aware of the nodes inside a cluster, but all that Spark now sees is a multitude of containers that are available to it, each with some set of resources. The YARN ApplicationMaster handles communication between the containers, taking the role of the Spark Master in Spark Standalone mode. It thus handles communication between worker nodes.

Each Executor in Spark runs within its own YARN container, each container itself residing within the general set of resources allocated by the ResourceManager per node. As with Spark standalone, one or more tasks will run inside of each YARN Container. Figure 2-10 shows how Spark executes within a YARN environment, as well as some of the relevant configuration parameters, which we will look at in more detail later.

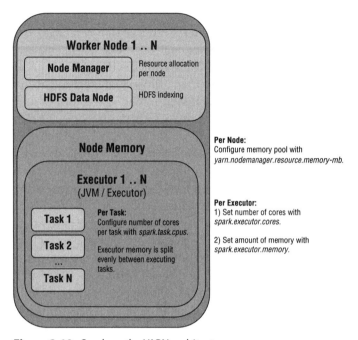

Figure 2-10: Spark on the YARN architecture

Let's next take a look at the actual structure of memory within the YARN container. When we discussed the internals of Spark, we saw how Spark structures its available memory in general, now we can see how this is specifically implemented within a cluster manager.

There are two YARN specific parameters shown in Figure 2-11 that are particularly important. The first of these is the `spark.yarn.executor` `.memoryOverhead` parameter. This is the parameter that the system uses to allocate additional memory for off-heap storage. Thus, when you allocate 8 GB of memory with `spark.executor.memory`, YARN actually allocates a container larger than that by the `spark.yarn.executor.memoryOverhead` parameter, by default the max of 384 or 10% of the `spark.executor.memory` parameter.

When the Spark driver is executed in cluster-mode (deployed as a separate process within the cluster rather than running on the host machine), Spark also supports configuring the `spark.yarn.driver.memoryOverhead` parameter, which dictates the memory available to the driver for off-heap storage. Note that these parameters, both for the driver and for individual executors, which define off-heap storage, are defaults, but these are not static allocations. The amount of memory consumed by an executor may actually change as the program runs depending on off-heap usage. Typically, in most programs, this will vary between 6% and 10% of the total utilized memory.

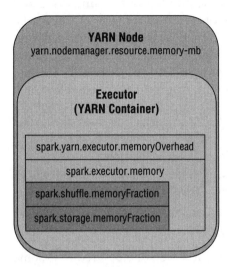

Figure 2-11: The YARN Container memory structure

External to this, are two YARN-specific parameters that control the total memory and CPU usage (not shown in the diagram) of YARN per node. These are configured within YARN, not within Spark. The `yarn.nodemanager` `.resource.memory-mb` dictates the total available memory for YARN containers per node and the `yarn.nodemanager.resource.cpu-vcores` controls the number of CPU cores available for YARN applications.

Dynamic Resource Allocation

In Spark Standalone, when you start a Spark cluster, the cluster manager pre-allocates a set of resources and instantiates each executor with these resources. Generally, the same thing happens when running Spark on YARN. However, this is obviously an inefficient use of resources; since a lot of the time these executors will be idle, not every job will require all available resources. Moreover, containers cannot be de-allocated until the job completes. This effectively makes some Spark applications resource hogs on a cluster, and, ultimately, not good cluster citizens. Especially for long-running jobs, this can become a problem with resources remaining blocked indefinitely.

Thus, in newer versions of Spark (1.2+) you can actually dynamically allocate and de-allocate resources for executors as necessary. Because YARN is a dynamic manager, rather than a static one like Spark Standalone, this approach lets us more efficiently use cluster resources. Dynamic resource management is presently limited to YARN deployments, neither Spark Standalone nor Mesos supports it.

With dynamic resource allocation enabled, Spark uses a set of heuristics to determine whether there is an excess of executors or whether more executors are needed. The first metric is whether there is a backlog of tasks waiting to be scheduled. Spark will periodically check the number of pending tasks and allocate an exponentially increasing number of executors if there continue to be pending tasks. An application will first add 1, then 2, then 4, and then 8 executors with the understanding that in most cases, a small number of executors will be sufficient. There is, however, a heavy workload, so it should ramp up quickly to keep up with demand. The following configurations are relevant.

- A request for additional resources comes when there have been pending tasks for at least `spark.dynamicAllocation.schedulerBacklogTimeout` seconds.

- The request repeats as long as pending tasks remain for every `spark.dynamicAllocation.sustainedSchedulerBacklogTimeout` seconds.

- When recovering resources, Spark simply de-allocates executors that have been idle for `spark.dynamicAllocation.executorIdleTimeout` seconds.

Enabling dynamic resource allocation takes a few steps, since it requires some manual cluster configuration. The following steps are replicated with slight modification from the Spark documentation:

1. Build Spark with the YARN profile. Skip this step if you are using a pre-packaged distribution.

2. Locate the `spark-<version>-yarn-shuffle.jar`. This should be under `$SPARK_HOME/network/yarn/target/scala-<version>` if you are building Spark yourself, and under `lib` if you are using a distribution.

3. Add this JAR to the classpath of all `NodeManagers` in your cluster.

4. In the `yarn-site.xml` on each node, add `spark_shuffle` to `yarn.nodemanager.aux-services`.

5. In the `yarn-site.xml` on each node, set `yarn.nodemanager.aux.services.spark_shuffle.class` to `org.apache.spark.network.yarn.YarnShuffleService`.

6. Set `spark.shuffle.service.enabled true`.

7. Set `spark.dynamicAllocation.enabled true`.

8. Restart all `NodeManagers` in your cluster.

With dynamic allocation enabled, you no longer have to manually set the `-num-executors` property because the system automatically scales the number of available executors to run tasks based on the demands of the scheduler. In earlier Spark versions (before 1.5), there is a known issue where cached RDDs may be retired when their associated containers are de-allocated. When working in the Spark shell and pausing between commands, cached RDDs may thus disappear.

Scenario

Now that we understand the architecture of a YARN deployment, let's actually look at a setup and execution of a Spark job on YARN. There are two options for running Spark on YARN. In the first case, the Driver runs on the machine that starts the Spark application, whether it is the spark-shell or a binary submitted with spark-submit. In this scenario, the YARN Application Master is only responsible for requesting resources from YARN, which is known as yarn-client mode. Alternately, the driver may itself be run within a YARN container, and the client may disconnect from the cluster or be used for other jobs. This is referred to as `yarn-cluster` mode.

A simple example running a job in `yarn-cluster` is shown here:

```
$SPARK_HOME/bin/spark-submit --master yarn-cluster --num-executors 4 ↵
--executor-cores 3 --class Main.class MyJar.jar
```

Alternately, we can run a Spark shell on yarn with:

```
$SPARK_HOME/bin/spark-shell --master yarn-client --num-executors 4 ↵
--executor-cores 3
```

We can see active YARN jobs through the YARN Resource Manager UI, as shown in Figure 2-12.

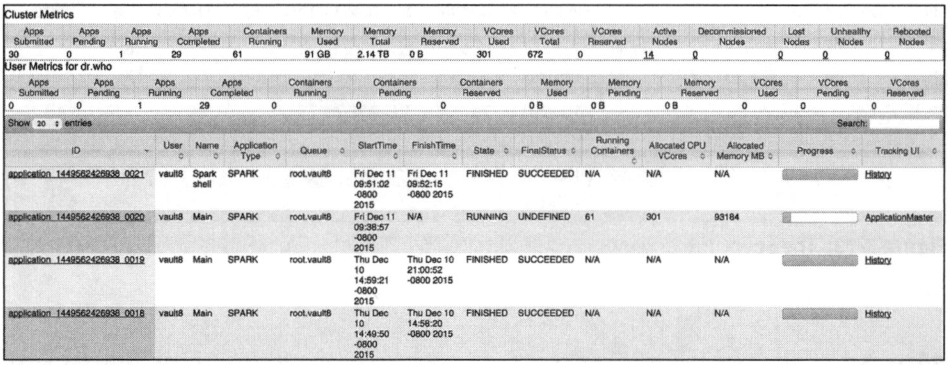

Figure 2-12: The YARN Job UI

This is fairly straightforward and that's really the idea! There are, however, complications that can arise from running on YARN. A common problem is that the YARN resource manager enforces certain constraints on its interaction with Spark. For example, when launching a Spark application you may attempt to allocate more resources than are available in the cluster with YARN. In this case, Spark will make a request, and rather than denying the request outright, YARN will wait for resources to become available, even if there may never be enough resources!

Another common problem is that the resources available to a single YARN container are fixed. Even though it's possible for more containers to be allocated, as we saw earlier, any individual container has a finite number of resources. The problem that arises is when a Spark application, for one reason or another, exceeds the memory available within a YARN container. This can happen due to ingesting too much data and attempting to operate on it in memory, or due to the outcome of a particular transformation. What happens in this case is that YARN will terminate the container and throw an error, but the underlying cause of the issue can be tricky to track down. Being aware of this potentiality helps identify it when it does happen and to know to look elsewhere for the root cause of the problem. In general, the Spark Job UI (Figure 2-13) is a good place to start when it comes to identifying execution errors and tracking them down.

Figure 2-13: The Spark Job UI view

Mesos

Mesos is an alternative to YARN with the primary advantage that it's not bound to the Hadoop ecosystem. Given that a large data center may contain multiple deployments, some running Hadoop, and some not, Mesos distinguishes itself in that it can manage the resources for the entire cluster. However, while Mesos is a standalone entity that fulfills a similar role to YARN, they are not mutually exclusive, nor do they really compete directly. YARN evolved alongside Hadoop MapReduce and, as such, is optimized for efficiently allocating resources for long-running batch jobs. Thus, YARN can efficiently schedule and manage a multitude of long-running large workloads but is less suitable for short-lived processing or long-running services, which may need to scale up and down.

Mesos, in contrast, because of its architecture, is somewhat more scalable and dynamic and as such can adapt better to short-lived workloads. Because Spark is a flexible framework that supports both long-lived large batch jobs as well as short-lived requests and persistent services, which service you select really depends on your use case and how you are using the tool. The good news is that if the situation requires, you can actually run both Mesos and YARN within the same environment.

To run both frameworks, nominally you would have to statically allocate resources—some for YARN, and some for Mesos, obviously a sub-optimal scenario. Because of the desire to unify these separate capabilities, a recent project has sought to bring these into a single framework. MapR, eBay, Twitter, and Mesosphere have collaborated to create Project Myriad that combines the functionality of Mesos and YARN. Myriad is an open-source project that essentially transforms YARN into a client of Mesos, allowing YARN to be more dynamic, while preserving its innate support for the Hadoop ecosystem.

In most cases, either Mesos or YARN will be more than sufficient to run a Spark cluster on their own, but Spark is part of a bigger picture and it's important to not lose sight of that. With that, let's look into the Architecture of Mesos.

Setup

To install Mesos in a Unix environment, first download the latest stable release where <version> is the version of Mesos you wish to use.

```
wget http://www.apache.org/dist/mesos/<version>/mesos-<version>.tar.gz
```

Extract it with:

```
tar -xvf mesos-<version>.tar.gz
```

Then, build with:

```
cd mesos
mkdir build
cd build
../configure
make
```

Mesos is now ready to go, but you'll need to repeat this process on each machine in the cluster. On the master node run (ensure that the working directory exists):

```
./bin/mesos-master.sh --ip=$MASTER_IP --work_dir=/var/lib/mesos
```

On the slaves, run:

```
./bin/mesos-slave.sh —master=$MASTER_IP:5050
```

And you can see the Mesos UI (Figure 2-14) at:

```
http://$MASTER_IP:5050.
```

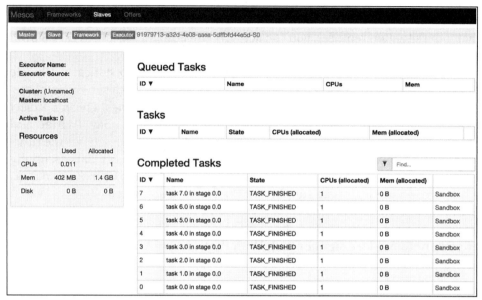

Figure 2-14: The Mesos UI

Architecture

Mesos runs as a separate set of processes on the cluster with the purpose of providing fine-grained allocation of resources. There are a number of differences between YARN's and Mesos' approach to resource allocation and we will cover some of them here. YARN is really a monolithic scheduler. Its approach is to allow frameworks to request resources. YARN then analyzes the available resources and assigns a chunk of them to the framework and runs the requested job. In contrast, when a framework submits a request to Mesos, things happen differently.

Like YARN, Mesos will analyze the available resources. However, at this point, instead of directly assigning a set of resources to the framework, Mesos instead provides a set of resource *offers* back to the requesting framework. It's then the responsibility of the framework to accept or deny these offers. The advantage of this approach is that each requesting framework now has the option of scheduling its jobs in a more fine-grained way. Mesos handles the strategic allocation of resources to ensure that they are fairly distributed based on rules and configurations, but the ultimate decision of how to use those resources becomes a function of the framework and the scheduler that it runs. This approach is thus more scalable, and more flexible since there is a continuous negotiation of resources between the framework and the Mesos master (see Figure 2-15).

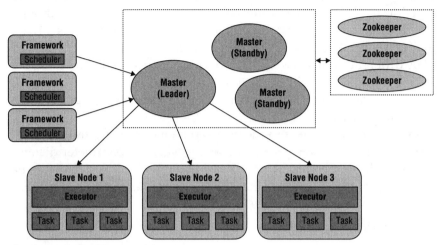

Figure 2-15: The Mesos architecture

Once a scheduler within the framework accepts the resource offer, the framework then sends the master a description of the tasks it wishes to run within the offered resources, and the Master launches the tasks on the corresponding slaves. Like with YARN, a Slave node may run multiple executors, each running multiple tasks. The Mesos architecture is redundant—standby nodes back the Mesos master and can replace it if it fails. Zookeeper is used to track the status of nodes in the cluster, like in YARN, and restart failed nodes.

When running Spark on Mesos, Spark is simply another framework. Mesos handles resource assignment for Spark at the task level. As the driver creates jobs and submits tasks to Mesos, Mesos dynamically assigns resources to handle these short-lived processes. Spark on Mesos supports both cluster-mode and client-mode like in YARN. In cluster-mode, the driver process runs within a resource block on the cluster and client-mode, where the Spark framework and driver remain on the machine launching the Spark job.

Spark on Mesos also offers two different operational modes for resource assignment. In the default fine-grained mode, there is a one-to-one mapping of Spark tasks to Mesos tasks. In this mode, overall resource usage is reduced but there is additional overhead of allocation/de-allocation of resources. As an alternative, Spark can run in coarse-grained mode where it runs a single long-running task on each Mesos machine and handles individual task scheduling within that machine. This approach is actually similar to how Spark Standalone works, except instead of manually handling cluster creation, Spark relies on Mesos for the initial assignment of resources. In coarse-grained mode, we benefit from lower overhead and quicker scheduling of short queries but sacrifice the dynamic nature of Mesos at its full potential.

Like with YARN, there exist additional Mesos-specific configuration parameters that it's important to understand. In fine-grained mode, one can configure the number of cores used per executor. Even though Mesos assigns resources on-demand, Mesos still allocates resources at the executor level (even though there is one Mesos task per Spark task). Thus each executor receives a fixed allocation of cores dictated by `spark.mesos.mesosExecutor.cores`, which may be shared by different Mesos tasks. The important distinction is that these are Mesos specific cores; Mesos still allocates additional cores based on the Spark `--executor-cores` parameter. Even when no Spark tasks are assigned, these Mesos cores remain active.

In addition, there is an analog to the off-heap memory configuration available in yarn. The `spark.mesos.executor.memoryOverhead` parameter dictates the additional off-heap memory available and like with YARN, defaults to be at least 384 or 10% of the `spark.executor.memory` parameter.

Dynamic Resource Allocation

Spark has some support for dynamic resource allocation using Mesos. Dynamic resource allocation using Mesos allows Spark to dynamically scale the number of executors when running in coarse-grained mode. In fine-grained mode, as we discussed earlier, Mesos will launch a single task for every Spark task and allow dynamic scaling of available resources. However, if we want to take advantage of the lower overhead of coarse-grained mode but still have the flexibility to adjust the resources used by Spark, then we can configure dynamic resource allocation.

To enable this setting we need to run the Mesos Shuffle Service, which handles shuffle cleanup. We do this by running the `$SPARK_HOME/sbin/start-mesos-shuffle-service.sh` script on each slave node that will run Spark executors.

Next, as with YARN, set `spark.dynamicAllocation.enabled true`.

- A request for additional resources comes when there have been pending tasks for at least `spark.dynamicAllocation.schedulerBacklogTimeout` seconds.
- The request repeats as long as pending tasks remain every `spark.dynamicAllocation.sustainedSchedulerBacklogTimeout` seconds.

When recovering resources, Spark simply de-allocates executors that have been idle for `spark.dynamicAllocation.executorIdleTimeout` seconds.

Basic Setup Scenario

As a sanity check, let's first make sure that everything in Mesos is running correctly. We've already started the master and slaves during the setup so let's just run a Java and a Python example with:

```
cd $MESOS_HOME
make check
$MESOS_HOME/src/examples/java/test-framework $MASTER_IP:5050
$MESOS_HOME/src/examples/python/test-framework $MASTER_IP:5050
```

To run Spark on Mesos, each slave must have a Spark binary package on a Hadoop-accessible URI, either `http://`, `s3n://`, or `hdfs://`.

Client Mode

Next, let's launch Spark in client-mode. First, we need to configure the `spark-env.sh` file on the driver to work properly with Mesos:

```
export MESOS_NATIVE_JAVA_LIBRARY=<path to libmesos.so>

export SPARK_EXECUTOR_URI=<path to Spark binary above>
```

> **NOTE** `libmesos.so` **is typically found in** `/usr/local/lib/libmesos.so`. **On Mac OS X it is instead** `libmesos.dylib`.

In the Spark configuration file or in the Spark context settings set:

```
spark.executor.uri <path to Spark binary above>
```

When creating a Spark Context, you must also set the master to point to the Mesos master:

```
val conf = new SparkConf()
.setMaster("mesos://$MASTER_IP:5050")
.set("spark.executor.uri", <path to Spark binary>)
val sc = new SparkContext(conf)
```

You can launch a shell with:

```
$SPARK_HOME/bin/spark-shell --master mesos://$MASTER_IP:5050
```

Cluster Mode

In cluster mode, the driver runs as a process within Mesos. To launch in cluster mode you must run:

```
$SPARK_HOME/sbin/start-mesos-dispatcher.sh $MASTER_IP:5050
```

You can then submit jobs with:

```
$SPARK_HOME/bin/spark-submit --master mesos://dispatcher:7077 ⏎
--num-executors 4 --executor-cores 3 ⏎
--class Main.class MyJar.jar
```

Fine-Grained versus Coarse-Grained Mode

Configuring the resource mode is straightforward. This is simply a property set in the spark configuration.

```
val conf = new SparkConf().set("spark.mesos.coarse", "true")
val sc = new SparkContext(conf)
```

When configuring coarse-grained scheduling, Spark will, by default, subsume all resources available to Mesos. Given that this is likely not what you want, particularly if you enable dynamic resource allocation, you can set the default number of cores with:

```
conf.set("spark.cores.max", "15")
```

Comparison

We've now introduced three unique ways of configuring and launching Spark jobs in a cluster. In this section, we'll review the differences between these frameworks and discuss the tradeoffs between them with the goal of helping you select the optimal solution.

Spark Standalone was the first option that we considered. Spark standalone offers a simple way to stand up a Spark cluster on multiple machines and has a substantial advantage of requiring no additional dependencies. Additionally, configuration, although it requires full access to the environment, is not overly complex.

The primary limitation of Spark Standalone is of course that it is not a true resource manager, and thus it is incapable of dynamically adjusting resource usage or flexibly handling concurrent usage. While you may have multiple concurrent users of a Spark Standalone cluster, it requires each application to explicitly and statically specify the number of resources it will consume, and thus requires coordination and collaboration between all users of this cluster. This is not an environment that readily supports the addition of new workloads and that can adjust to changes in the demands of individual applications.

From a performance perspective, Spark Standalone is the simplest of all the frameworks and pre-allocates all resources used by Spark; thus, it has the lowest startup time when it comes to launching a new Spark application.

The next framework we looked at was YARN. YARN offers a much more flexible approach to cluster management and helps address many of the limitations of Spark Standalone. Even in its default mode, without dynamic resource allocation, YARN provides a more robust framework for running a cluster and facilitates multi-tenancy and scalable resource management.

First and foremost, because resource usage and scheduling in YARN is strictly controlled and allocated, via queues and user profiles, it's much more straightforward to independently handle resource sharing in a cluster between multiple concurrent users. Multiple users do not need to coordinate their application's resource usage or their resource allocation strategy. Instead, their available resources are configurable and ultimately controlled by the cluster administrator. The cluster administrator is thus able to ensure fair resource distribution between multiple users by configuring YARN appropriately and letting the framework solve the more complex challenge of scheduling and resource sharing (see Figure 2-16).

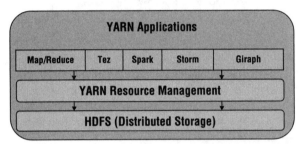

Figure 2-16: Concurrent applications and services on YARN

In Spark Standalone, when launching a cluster, one must explicitly specify the resources allocated to the cluster on a per-machine basis. This static allocation is persistent and cannot be adjusted later. The impact of this is two-fold. First, you can't dynamically scale up the resources available to the cluster—as cluster usage increases, there will not be any way to scale up to meet the increased demand without downtime. Second, this static allocation permanently limits the resources available to all other applications running on those machines as long as the Spark Standalone cluster is active.

YARN addresses both of these limitations directly. There is no static allocation of resources for a YARN cluster. Instead, you can elastically scale up and or scale down, adding machines and resources on demand without downtime. Transparently to the user, YARN will allocate new jobs on the physical resources available. Newer versions of Hadoop support high-availability and support fail-over meaning that it's possible to add new machines to the Hadoop cluster and increase the overall pool of physical resources available without cluster downtime. Thus, applications can continue to run without being interrupted, providing a better user experience and ensuring business continuity.

Secondly, resource usage in YARN is not static. As applications arrive, execute, and complete, they release the resources that they use back into the pool of available resources. There is no permanent allocation of resources within YARN allowing load and resource usage to scale elastically as different kinds and numbers of applications execute on a YARN cluster. In periods of heavy load, resource intensive applications may be forced to wait for resources to become available but they will never be forced to wait indefinitely because of this dynamic allocation of resources (see Figure 2-17).

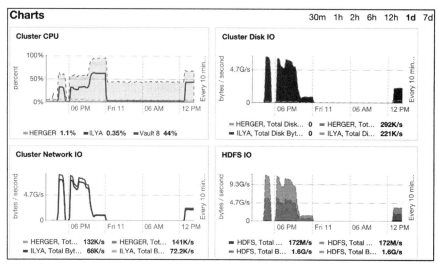

Figure 2-17: Dynamic resource usage on a YARN cluster

In addition to the advantages we've already discussed, YARN's support of dynamic resource usage within Spark affords an even greater level of flexibility and allows Spark on YARN to be a better cluster citizen. Long-lived and resource intensive applications can configure dynamic resource allocation to release some of the resources they require back to YARN for use by other applications (see Figure 2-18).

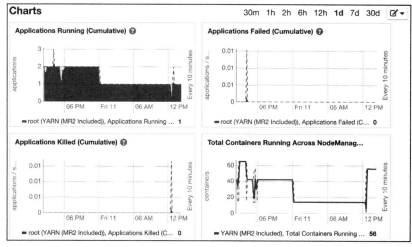

Figure 2-18: Dynamic application and container usage with YARN

There are two major shortcomings of Spark on YARN. In practical scenarios, the major issue is that Spark may exceed the resources allocated to it by YARN causing errors that are usually difficult to track down and isolate. Running large and complex Spark applications on YARN thus demands intimate familiarity with the core architecture of Spark and the knowledge of how to configure Spark applications for reliability and proper resource usage.

The second challenge is simply one of complexity—there are more moving pieces involved in standing up and maintaining a YARN cluster. Adding the dependency on Hadoop and YARN as additional components introduces more points of failure and potential challenges with regards to upgradeability and configuration.

There are also conflicting resource demands from multiple users and applications—thus occasionally making it more challenging or slower to run any one application. While YARN balances these demands, and ensures that everything runs smoothly, YARN cannot guarantee that any one application will run as quickly or efficiently as it would if it could consume all available resources. For simple use cases, Spark standalone tends to be the better option, and should likely be used unless the use case explicitly demands the greater flexibility and dynamism of YARN.

The final framework that we considered was Mesos. Mesos provides many of the same advantages over Spark standalone as YARN. It likewise affords greater flexibility with regards to multi-tenancy and shared cluster usage. Mesos also supports dynamic allocation of resources and elastic scaling of available resources within a cluster. Thus, for highly dynamic applications or for more general workloads, Mesos is frequently the cluster management tool of choice. Spark was also originally developed on Mesos (until Spark standalone evolved as a sustainable option). Although Spark is now more frequently deployed on YARN, a shared experience across many use cases suggests that it's easier to reliably run larger Spark workloads within Mesos than within YARN.

One major advantage of Mesos over YARN is that Mesos allows you to explicitly make tradeoffs in resource allocation strategies to either help Spark be a better cluster citizen or to improve the responsiveness of long-lived Spark services and applications. Because Mesos allows us to configure the granularity of resource allocation, you can choose between allowing better overall resource management in fine-grained mode or to reduce the runtime cost of launching new Spark applications and tasks with coarse-grained allocation mode.

Mesos is also arguably more scalable than YARN since it does not have a single bottleneck for scheduling and resource allocation as YARN does. Moreover, Mesos' approach to letting applications choose the resources that they ultimately use supports a more robust resource allocation strategy, and as Spark continues to evolve as a technology, supports a broader variety of use cases and more advanced resource scheduling. Lastly, because Mesos does not depend on Hadoop, it's potentially adaptable to a much wider variety of use cases since not all Spark clusters are based on the Hadoop ecosystem.

Where Mesos trails behind YARN is in some of the more advanced features for cluster configuration. For example, because of YARN's centralized control model, YARN supports enforcing global resource constraints, like the resources available to users within a group, without sacrificing the ability to explicitly configure rack and node locality settings. YARN also hides a lot of the heavy lifting when it comes to deploying dependencies such as libraries and jars or security tokens to individual nodes and containers within the environment.

Summary

In this chapter we learned about the importance of cluster management. We learned about the challenges associated with creating an environment where many concurrent users and applications compete for a shared pool of available resources, and how frameworks like YARN and Mesos can reliably handle this conflict of interests to ensure that all applications and users have fair access to these resources. We also established how these frameworks evolved as a generalization of the operating systems that handle resource allocation and scheduling on a single machine, allowing us to better understand the role of a cluster management tool in the broader data ecosystem.

We introduced Spark Standalone as the simplest tool for cluster management of a Spark environment. Spark Standalone pre-allocates a set of resources for Spark jobs and while this allows for rapid execution and launching of Spark jobs, it does not provide an optimal allocation of resources in the cluster and does not support a number of critical use cases. Specifically, with Spark Standalone one cannot dynamically adjust the number of resources available in a cluster, nor can one readily share resources between multiple applications.

To address some of these limitations, Spark also supports execution on two other frameworks for cluster management. The first of these is YARN, the resource manager for the Hadoop ecosystem. As Hadoop's popularity and adoption has grown, Spark on YARN has become increasingly common in many enterprises. YARN allows Spark to plug transparently into the broader Hadoop ecosystem, allowing it to run in tandem with a wide variety of other applications and lets users utilize a variety of tools to tackle the problems they're faced with. YARN provides users with the flexibility to use tools that address a much broader set of use cases than Spark can support on its own.

YARN allows Spark to move from a model based around static allocation of resources to a much more dynamic approach of requesting and releasing resources on demand. This lets Spark share the resources of a cluster while allowing users to write Spark applications that may adjust their resource usage over time—allowing for greater dynamism and support of a broader set of solutions. YARN also supports elastic scaling of resources in a cluster, making it possible to add new resources as they become necessary, facilitating long-term growth for businesses and projects. This ability to scale out hardware resources dynamically allows the same application to be run against increasingly larger dataset(s) without needing to fundamentally rewrite the application, or the architecture that executes it.

Lastly, we looked at Mesos—a more general-purpose framework for resource management that is not tied to the Hadoop ecosystem. Mesos has a number of advantages over YARN in that it allows more control over the resource allocation policy, letting the user optimize Spark applications depending on whether they are short-lived or long-lived, and it provides a more flexible scheduling policy for the applications, such as Spark, that use it.

Although there are distinctions between Mesos and YARN, as we discussed in the previous section, in most practical use cases these will be interchangeable with regards to performance and ease of use. Moreover, unless Mesos and YARN are often necessary, Spark Standalone offers you the easiest way to get up and running and have a functional Spark cluster. Ultimately, which resource and cluster management tool you select will be a function of your use case.

Performance Tuning

In the previous two chapters we followed the steps necessary to make a Spark application run on top of a stable production environment. But those steps alone are not enough—we still want to do more to get the best out of the application. Even though Spark, as a cluster computing framework, capably deals with the major problems that distributed processing is involved with, such as scalability, fault tolerance, job scheduling, load balancing, and so on, the task of writing efficient code that can run distributed across a cluster is not trivial. We always risk encountering performance bottlenecks.

In this chapter we will explore several techniques to improve the performance of Spark jobs and to avoid potential bottlenecks. Understanding Spark's fundamentals is the first thing you must do in order to write efficient jobs.

With performance in mind, in this chapter we start by tackling Spark's execution model, describing the way data is being shuffled. We will see why we should avoid data shuffling, and when it is a good time to do it. We will also explain why partitioning is important and how efficiency is impacted by the way we choose to use the Spark operators.

We will also include a section in this chapter dedicated to data serialization that evaluates the supported serializers: Java and Kryo.

An important player that improves a Spark application's performance is the caching mechanism. Saving intermediary results or tables in memory can preserve a considerable amount of time that would otherwise have been spent recomputing an RDD or loading data from a disk. This chapter describes how to make use of the Spark cache. Because the Spark SQL cache has a special behavior, we will also include a section dedicated to the way tables are cached, in order to obtain a better performance.

Spark is famous for being an in-memory engine for large-scale data processing but do you know what "in-memory" really means? When does Spark use memory? In the following pages we will answer these questions, look at the situations in which Spark makes great use of memory, and how garbage collection impacts the performance.

In this chapter we will also familiarize you with the two types of shared variables:

- The broadcasted variables used to efficiently distribute large values across the cluster
- The accumulator variables used for aggregating information from workers

We will discuss when to use them and why they are meaningful to our distributed applications. We will conclude this chapter with a few words about data locality, describing how Spark takes advantage of data proximity to increase the execution performance, and how can you control this behavior.

Spark Execution Model

Before diving into performance improvements it is essential to increase your fundamental knowledge about how Spark executes programs in a distributed fashion across a cluster. When you are running a Spark application, a driver process is launched alongside a series of executor processes that are distributed on the worker nodes across the cluster. The driver program has the responsibility of running the user application and of managing all of the work that needs to be executed when an action is triggered. On the other hand, the executor processes are the ones that perform the actual work in the form of tasks and save the results. But how do these tasks get to the executors?

For each action triggered inside of a Spark application, the DAG scheduler creates an execution plan to accomplish it. The conception of this execution plan consists of assembling as many transformations with *narrow dependencies* as possible into stages. A narrow dependency between RDDs is when each partition from the parent RDD is used at most by a single partition from the child RDD. A stage finds its limit when you have some *wide dependencies* that require shuffle operations. A wide dependency between RDDs happens when a partition of the parent's RDD is used by multiple child RDD partitions (see Figure 3-1).

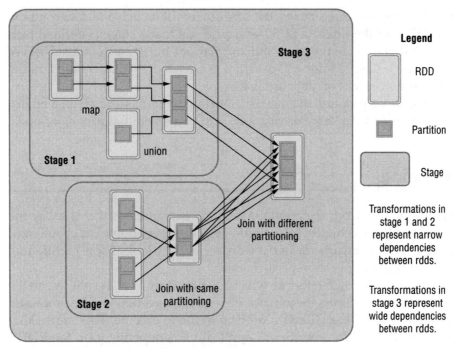

Figure 3-1: Wide and narrow RDD dependencies

Let's look at an example of this. Consider the following code snippet:

```
val numbers = sc.parallelize(nrCollection)
val multiplied = numbers.filter(_%2 == 0).map(_ * 3).collect()
```

The previous code filters the even numbers, then multiplies them by 3 and executes the action of collecting them. These are all narrow transformations because their input partition data is not distributed in multiple output partitions, so all of them will be executed in the same stage.

On the other hand, the following code will count the number of words inside of a file, filter the words that appear exactly 10 times, and then count each character appearance within these words. In the end a `collect` action will trigger the job execution. Within these transformations there are two of them that are stage boundaries (they have wide dependencies). The two `reduceByKey` transformations are the reason why this code will generate three stages:

```
val words = sc.textFile("textFilePath").flatMap(_.split(' '))
val wordCounts = words.map((_, 1)).reduceByKey(_ + _)
val filteredWords = wordCounts.filter(_._2 == 10)
val characters = filteredWords.flatMap(_._1.toCharArray)
                 .map((_, 1)).reduceByKey(_ + _)
characters.collect()
```

After defining the three stages, the scheduler will launch a task to compute each partition of the final RDD. So we could say that a stage is defined by a set of tasks that execute the same transformations but on different subsets of the data. The task scheduler will assign these tasks to executors based on the available resources and on data locality.

For example if a partition that needs to be transformed is already in memory on a certain node, then the task execution will be sent on that particular node.

Partitioning

We can easily infer from the previous section's explanations that the way the RDDs are partitioned highly impacts the way the execution plan is built and therefore implicitly impacts the performance. Now let's look at how partitioning affects your Spark application performance.

The partitions are fragments into which the data in an RDD is split. When the DAG scheduler transforms the job into stages, each partition will be processed into a single task, with each task requiring a core to execute. This means that the parallelism level for your Spark application is dependent on the RDD's partition number. So it is easy to understand why this number is probably the most important thing to consider when tuning the performance of your Spark application.

Controlling Parallelism

The number of partitions for an RDD strongly depends on the way it was created. RDDs that are created over files have a default number of partitions. For example, if the files are stored on HDFS, the number of partitions will be equal to the number of blocks (one partition for each block of file). This means that you could control the number of partitions that will be created either by writing the files on HDFS in smaller or larger blocks, or configuring the InputFormat to create more or less splits.

You can also create an RDD by parallelizing a collection. In this case, the default number of partitions is given by the spark.default.parallelism property. This default value depends on the cluster manager: for Spark 1.5.2 run in local mode, it will be a number equal to the number of cores; for Mesos in fine-grained mode it will be 8; and in the other cases, it will be the maximum number between 2 and the total number of cores on all executors.

However, you can control these default values. For both RDD creation methods you can use a user input parameter that allows you to control the number of partitions:

```
sc.textFile(<inputPath>, <minPartitions>)
sc.parallelize(<sequence>, <numSlices>)
```

The most common way to create RDDs is to apply some transformations on already existing RDDs. Usually the partition number in an RDD is the same as the number of partitions from the RDD that it depends upon. However, some transformations, such as "union" will break this rule because it creates an RDD that has a number of partitions equal to the sum of the parent's partition number.

Let's look at another type of transformation, the one that causes data shuffling. These transformations are the ones that have wide dependencies, meaning that for computing one partition of an RDD you might need to process data from multiple partitions of the parent RDDs. In this case, the default number of partitions will be the largest number of partitions from the dependent RDDs, if not specified otherwise. Take as an example the groupByKey transformation applied on top of a Pair RDD:

```
rdd.groupByKey(<numTasks>)
```

Writing an efficient Spark application inevitably implies setting an optimal number of partitions. Imagine that the number of tasks spawned for your job is smaller than the number of available CPUs. In this case you might be facing two performance issues: First, you won't benefit from your entire computing power, and second, if the number of partitions is small, then the data inside of one partition will be larger than if you would have it distributed across a larger number of partitions. For large datasets, this will bring some memory pressure on a task and on garbage collection and, if this happens, the processing will be slowed down.

Also, if the data within one partition is too large to fit in memory, then it has to be spilled to disk in order to avoid out-of-memory exceptions. But spilling it to disk brings a huge overhead caused by sorting and disk I/O.

To benefit from the entirety of your computing power, you should have a number of partitions at least as high as the number of CPUs assigned to your application across the cluster. But this won't necessarily fix the problem of large partitions. If you have a huge dataset, and a fairly small cluster you will still have over-dimensioned partitions. In this case, the number of partitions for an RDD has to be higher than the number of available cores.

On the other hand, you have to be careful not to end up at the other extreme, that is, you must not set too many partitions. Setting too many partitions will spawn lots of small tasks that would need to be sent to worker nodes to be executed. This will increase the overhead of scheduling tasks. However, the penalty of launching tasks is smaller than the one of spilling data to disk. One sign that your level of parallelism is too high is the fact that you have tasks that finish almost instantly, or they don't read or write anything.

It is hard to compute the best number of partitions for an RDD because it depends heavily on the dataset's size, on the partitioner itself, and on the total amount of memory available for each task. To be able to estimate a fairly accurate number you have to know your data and its distribution well. However, the recommended number of partitions per RDD would be the number of CPUs multiplied by 2 to 4.

Partitioners

We covered how you can control the number of partitions inside of an RDD, but what about the way the data is distributed across these partitions? To scatter the data in partitions across the cluster, Spark uses partitioners. These two already-built partitioners are called `HashPartitioner` and `RangePartitioner`.

The default behavior for choosing the partitioner for operations that require the setting of a partitioner follows one of these two parameters:

1. If any of the input RDDs has a partitioner, then the output RDD is partitioned using that particular one.

2. Otherwise, in case of the pair RDDs, the `HashPartitioner` is used by default.

The `HashPartitioner` distributes the values across partitions based on the key hash code. The partition index is identified by computing the key's hash code modulo the number of partitions, taking into account the sign of the hash code.

The `RangePartitioner` partitions sortable entries by range. Sampling the content of the RDD, it determines the ranges to be of approximately equal size. The final number of partitions might be smaller than the configured number.

However, you are not limited to these partitioners. You can write your own custom one. This is useful when you have a good working knowledge of the domain of your use case. For example, let's assume you have a pair of RDDs, where the keys are file paths on a file system. If you use the `HashPartitioner`, the `folder1/firstFileName.txt` and `folder1/secondFileName.png` might end up in different partitions on different nodes. If you want all of the files in a folder to be in the same partition, you could write your own partitioner that distributes the files based on the parent folder.

Writing a custom partitioner is fairly easy. You just have to extend the partitioner "org.apache.spark.Partitioner" and provide implementation for the following methods:

- `getPartition(key : Any) : Int`—to provide the partition ID for a certain key.

- `numPartitions: Int`—specify the number of partitions your partitioner creates.

- `equals and hashcode`—methods to be used to test your partitioner against other partitioners.

Once implemented, a custom partitioner is easy to use. You either pass it to the `partitionBy` function or to the shuffle based functions:

```
pairRdd.partitionBy(new MyPartitioner(3))
firstPairRdd.join(secondPairRdd, new MyPartitioner(3))
```

Some operations, such as the map function affect partitioning. During a map operation you can change the keys inside a pair RDD so the partitioning won't remain the same. In this case, the resulted RDD won't have a partitioner set. However, you can use one of two alternatives to map the values inside a pair RDD and keep the partitioner: `mapValues` and `flatMapValues`.

Shuffling Data

When you are dealing with data in a distributed fashion, you will often perform map and reduce transformations. These transformations are expensive as the reduce phase assumes a data shuffling step. This operation is not a trivial one as large chunks of data have to be sent from one node to another, stressing the CPU, disk, memory, and of course, the network capacities of the cluster.

This process is expensive because it can involve data sorting and repartitioning, serialization and deserialization while sending it over the network, and data compression to reduce the I/O bandwidth and disk I/O operations.

To understand the importance of the shuffling stage we will cover the operations performed during this phase.

In Spark, each map tasks (M) writes its output in a shuffle file (one file per reducer R) to disk. Because you might have a lot of mappers and reducers the number of shuffle files (M*R) might be significantly large (see Figure 3-2). This is a major reason why you have performance loss. However, just like in Hadoop, you have the possibility to compress these output files by setting the `spark.shuffle .compress` parameter to true. The library used for compression is also configurable through the `spark.io.compression.codec` property. By default in Spark 1.5.2, the snappy compression will be used but you can choose between lz4, lzf, and snappy. Using compression is a tradeoff, however; you gain in terms of disk IO, but you lose in terms of memory. Compressing the mapper's output files might lead to memory pressure, of course, depending on the compression library you chose.

In the reduce phase you may also face memory problems because all of the shuffled data for a reducer task has to fit in memory. If it doesn't fit, then an out-of-memory exception is thrown and the entire job will fail. This is why the number of reducers is very important. When you have more reducers you will decrease the amount of data per reducer.

Unlike Hadoop where the map and reduce phases overlap, and the mappers push their output to reducers, in Spark the reduce phase starts only when the map phase is finished. The reducers will then pull for the shuffled data. The network buffer size used for fetching the mapper's output is controlled through the `spark.reducer.maxSizeInFlight` parameter.

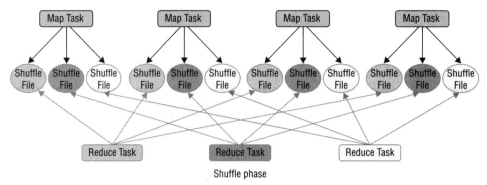

Figure 3-2: The Shuffle phase

As we mentioned earlier in this chapter, the map phase outputs a large amount of shuffle files (the number of mappers multiplied by the number of reducers), which leads to real stress on the operating system. In Spark you can possibly introduce an intermediary merge phase that will output fewer and larger files. This phase is called *shuffle file consolidation*. What happens is that the map phase outputs a shuffle file for each partition. The number of shuffle files will be the number of reducers per core instead of the number of reducers per mappers. All of the map tasks that run on the same core will output the same shuffle files, one for each reducer (see Figure 3-3). To enable shuffle file consolidation you have to set `spark.shuffle.consolidateFiles` to true.

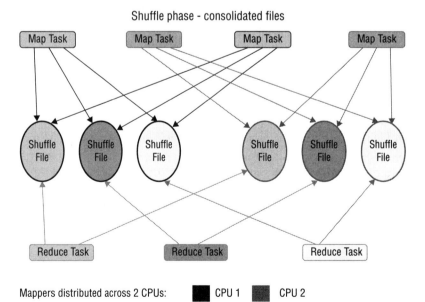

Figure 3-3: The Shuffle file consolidation phase

Shuffling and Data Partitioning

Many transformations require data shuffling across the cluster, including `join`, `reduceByKey`, `groupByKey`, `cogroup`, and so on. All of these operations can be very expensive because they might need the entire datasets to be shuffled, sorted, and repartitioned. But there is a "trick" you can use that will increase the performance: pre-partitioning. All of these transformations that depend on how the data is scattered across the cluster can benefit greatly from data partitioning.

If the RDDs are partitioned, data shuffling can be avoided. Let's take as an example the `reduceByKey` transformation—it is made on a single RDD:

```
xRdd.reduceByKey(_+_)
```

In this example, if the xRdd can't be partitioned, all of the data within it would have to be shuffled and sorted by key in order to be able to apply the sum function on the values of a certain key. On the other hand, if xRdd *is* partitioned, then all of the values for a certain key will be in the same partition, so they will be processed locally. In this way data shuffling across the network is avoided (see Figure 3-4).

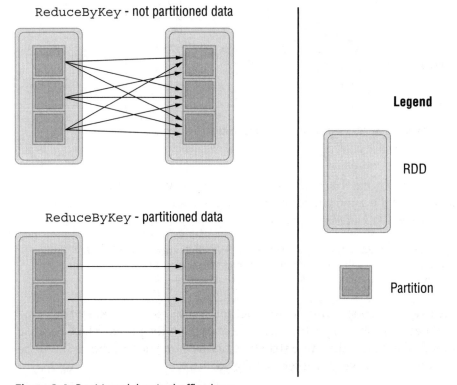

Figure 3-4: Partitioned date in shuffle phase

Data partitioning becomes even more important for transformations that involve two or more RDDs. The more RDDs you join, the more data will need to be processed, data that becomes the subject of shuffling. Consider the following example:

```
val partitionedRdd = pairRdd.partitionBy(new HashPartitioner(3))
val joinedRdd = partitionedRdd.join(otherRdd)
```

The previous code joins a partitioned RDD with another one that is not partitioned. In this case, the partitioned RDD is the one that will pass the partitioner to the resulted RDD. This RDD will be processed locally on each worker and only the one that is not partitioned will be sorted and shipped to the proper nodes (see Figure 3-5).

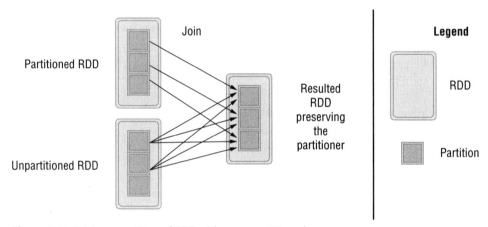

Figure 3-5: Joining a partitioned RDD with an unpartitioned one

To further improve the `join` transformation, you could have both RDDs partitioned with the same partitioner. In this case, none of these will be shuffled across the network. Here is an example:

```
val partitionedRdd = pairRdd.partitionBy(new HashPartitioner(3))
val otherRdd = partitionedRdd.mapValues(value => value + 1)
val joinedRdd = partitionedRdd.join(otherRdd)
```

In the previous code example, the method `mapValues` will keep the same partitioner and number of partitions as the ones from the parent RDD. Because both joined RDDs have the same structure on the same nodes, the data will be processed locally on every worker (see Figure 3-6).

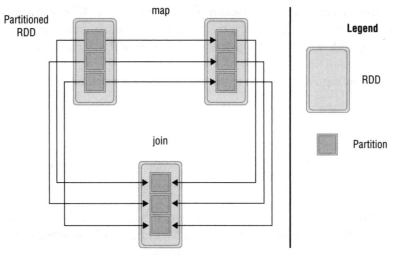

Figure 3-6: Joining two partitioned RDD

Let's summarize what we've covered thus far. Because shuffling is a highly expensive phase, the focus when you are writing Spark applications should be to decrease as much as possible the number of shuffles and the amount of data that gets shipped across the cluster. Properly partitioned RDDs can really boost the performance of your application because you avoid the entire overhead brought by shipping the data across nodes: CPU, disk, memory, and network I/O pressure.

Operators and Shuffling

Another way to avoid large amounts of data being scattered across the worker nodes, besides data partitioning, is to choose the right operators at the right time. This is a problem that many inexperienced Spark users face. We tend to use the transformations we need to get our job done, without considering what operations they trigger behind the curtains. This is one of the most common mistakes users make that impacts the performance of Spark applications.

Let's review some of the most frequent performance pitfalls. We will cover when to not use some transformations in certain situations as well as when it is the right time to take advantage of them. The scope is not to provide only some patterns but to raise awareness of the actions that the code triggers in order to make better decisions when choosing the transformation operations on your RDDs.

groupByKey versus reduceByKey

For those situations where we need to apply some functions on top of all of the values of a certain key, we have two options: the two Spark operators, reduceByKey and groupByKey. So when should you use one over the other?

Let's assume the classic word count example. We have an RDD containing a list of words and we want to count the number of times each word appears. We can solve this problem with both of the aforementioned operators so let's go through each solution and see what they show us.

Consider the following RDD, which contains tuples of a word and 1:

```
val words = Array ("one", "two", "one", "one", "one", "two", "two", ↵
"one", "one", "two", "two")
val wordsPairRdd = sc.parallelize(words).map(w => (w,1))
```

First, count the number of times each word appears using the `groupByKey` operator:

```
wordsPairRdd.groupByKey().map(t => (t._1, t._2.sum))
```

In this case, all of the values for a certain key must be processed in a single task. To accomplish this, the entire dataset is shuffled and all of the word pairs for a certain key are sent to a single node.

Apart from the time penalty inflicted by the entire data shuffling, you might face another issue: If you are processing a huge dataset where one key has a lot of values, you might use all of your memory on a task, and your job will fail with an out-of-memory exception.

The second way to solve the word count problem is to use the `reduceByKey`:

```
wordsPairRdd.reduceByKey(_ + _)
```

This time the function passed to the `reduceByKey` operator is applied to all of the values of a key on a single machine and only these intermediary results are then sent across the cluster (as shown in Figure 3-7).

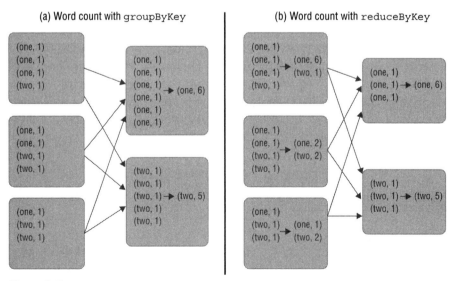

Figure 3-7: ReduceByKey versus groupByKey.

By using `reduceByKey` instead of `groupByKey` to solve this aggregation problem we significantly reduce the data that has to be compressed and shuffled, thereby gaining a huge performance improvement. This example illustrates that we should avoid `groupByKey` for associative and reductive operations.

repartition versus coalesce

We discussed the role partitioning plays in the execution time of a Spark application. We often encounter this situation when we have to change the number of partitions in our RDDs, to change the parallelism, for example. Two Spark operators help to accomplish this: repartition and coalesce. However, it is important to understand which of them to use.

The repartition operator randomly reshuffles the data and distributes it in a number of partitions that are either larger or smaller compared to RDD's initial number of partitions. You can also obtain the same result with the coalesce operator, but you can avoid shuffling if you dimension your RDD to a smaller number of partitions. The partitions on the same machine will be merged in order to obtain the desired number (see Figure 3-8).

It's important to know that shuffling is not always avoided on coalesce. If you severely decrease the number of partitions, setting it to a number smaller than the number of nodes, then the data on the extra nodes has to be sent to the other nodes containing the partitions (see Figure 3-8). When you decrease the number of partitions, the coalesce operator performs better than repartition because only a subset of your data is shuffled, not the entire dataset.

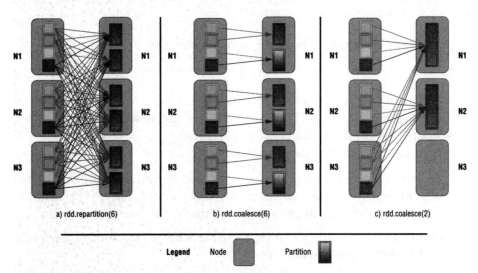

a) rdd.repartition(6)   b) rdd.coalesce(6)   c) rdd.coalesce(2)

Legend   Node   Partition

Figure 3-8: Changing the number of partitions, repartition versus coalesce

reduceByKey versus aggregateByKey

Let's assume you have a list of tuples that have keys as the user IDs and values as the sites a user has accessed at one point in time:

```
val userAccesses = sc.parallelize(Array(("u1", "site1"), ↵
("u1", "site2"), ("u1", "site1"), ("u2", "site3"), ("u2", "site4"), ↵
("u1", "site1")))
```

You want to process this list to obtain the unique sites a user has accessed. You have several options to do this. One of the possible solutions is to use `groupByKey()` and `distinct ()`. But as we already discussed, the `groupByKey` operator might shuffle the entire data across a cluster, so we will need a better option to solve this problem. So let's analyze other options we have: `reduceByKey` and `aggregateByKey`. To solve this problem using `reduceByKey`, you could write the following code:

```
val mapedUserAccess = userAccesses.map(userSite => (userSite._1, ↵
Set(userSite._2)))
val distinctSites = mapedUserAccess.reduceByKey(_ ++ _)
```

The first problem that we notice in the previous code is the fact that a new set is created for each value of this RDD. If you are processing a huge RDD, all of those objects will flood the memory and put pressure on the garbage collector that is trying to keep up with them.

What about `aggregateByKey`? Let's look at the following code:

```
val zeroValue = collection.mutable.Set[String]()
val aggredated = userAccesses.aggregateByKey (zeroValue)((set, v) => ↵
set += v, (setOne, setTwo) => setOne ++= setTwo)
```

If you collect the results of both solutions you obtain:

```
Array((u1,Set(site2, site1)), (u2,Set(site3, site4)))
```

To avoid all of the memory allocation that the `reduceByKey` solution has, you can use the `aggregateByKey`. This operator is slightly more difficult to use but once you understand it, you will find it easy to use.

You have to provide three parameters to this function:

1. **The zero value**—the initial value to be aggregated. In our example we chose an empty mutable set to collect the distinct values in it and not to affect the total values to be aggregated, thereby remaining neutral.

2. **A function** `f: (U, V)`—U to merge a value **V** into a structure U. This merging operation is made within a partition.

3. **A function** `g: (U, U)`—U that merges two structures of U. This function will be called when merging values between partitions.

To summarize, let's compare these two solutions. Aggregating by key is more efficient because we dodge the creation of a huge amount of objects, and we also skip an extra transformation step: the map step. To be able to reduce by key over the input RDD, we first have to map each element to a set containing only that element, which is time consuming for large datasets. Bottom line, use `aggregateByKey` when the value type changes. In terms of shuffle overhead, both solutions perform well because they both first apply the computation locally on each machine, and then shuffle the intermediary results across the cluster.

Shuffling Is Not That Bad After All

In the previous section of this chapter we covered all of the reasons why shuffling should be avoided and generally, this is a good advice. But not all shuffling is bad. In the first place, shuffling is a necessary operation because it is the way Spark reorganizes the data on your cluster.

Sometimes, the benefits of shuffling are higher than the overhead it inflicts. In the beginning of this chapter, we discussed how increasing the parallelism level could be a real performance booster. To increase or to decrease the parallelism in our Spark application we sometimes repartition our RDDs. In most of the cases, repartitioning requires data to be shuffled across the cluster. So in this case, we pay a price during shuffling, but we gain much more from the execution of all the processing with a proper parallelism.

Another important benefit to shuffling is that it can sometimes save the execution of your application. In the aggregation examples we provided earlier in this chapter we identified a potential risk: When your data is organized in a large number of partitions, you may face a bottleneck on the driver while trying to merge all the results. To relax the load on the driver a little, you could specify the number of partitions of the resulted RDD when calling the aggregation operator. We force a distributed aggregation this way—before sending the partial results on the driver:

```
rdd.reduceByKey(_ ++ _, 100)
```

Serialization

Because Spark is a distributed system it often needs to transfer data over the network, across the cluster, cache it in memory, or spill it to disk. Therefore, the way Spark serializes the objects representing your data, or the compression algorithm used for reducing its volume, really matters.

In Spark, your data records have two forms: either a serialized binary representation, or a deserialized Java object representation. Usually, Spark uses the deserialized representation when it handles your data in memory and only serializes it when shipping it between nodes across a network, or when it writes it to disk.

The serializer Spark uses for saving the state of your objects in a binary format is pluggable. By default, the standard Java serialization is used but you can also configure your application to use the Kryo serialization. Choosing the right serializer makes a huge difference in the performance of any distributed application because the processing might be greatly slowed if the serialization of your objects takes a lot of time or if it consumes a large number of bytes.

The default Java Serializer is able to serialize all of the objects that implement the Serializable interface. This option is slow and the objects of many classes end up being serialized in large formats. However, you can be more in control of your serialization's performance by implementing the Externalizable interface and provide your own way of saving and restoring the state of your object by implementing the `writeExternal` and `readExternal` methods.

The second supported serializer is a third-party serialization library. Kryo significantly improves the speed of the Java serializer and outputs a more compact binary representation of the objects. This serializer does not support all of the classes that implement Serializable.

When transforming an object into a binary representation, Kryo has to first write something that will identify the class of the object. So when serializing each record, the full class name will be written before the record itself. This becomes a problem when you have a lot of records because the data consumes more space and time. To improve performance you have to register your custom classes to this serializer. This means you need to know in advance the objects of which classes will be serialized. Knowing this, Kryo is able to map each class to an integer ID and write this ID before each record. It is more efficient to write an `int` value instead of the full class name.

To ensure you are always taking advantage of this improvement you can set the `spark.kryo.registrationRequired` property to true, which forces all of the classes that are serialized to be registered. You will receive an error if there is an attempt to serialize an unregistered class.

To change the serializer from the default Java one to Kryo you will have to set the following property:

```
val configuration = new SparkConf()
configuration.set("spark.serializer","org.apache.spark.serializer. ↵
KryoSerializer")
```

The serializer you set through this property will be used not only during the shuffle phase, but also when writing records to disk. It is highly recommended to use Kryo especially in network intensive applications as it is more efficient and improves performance. The only reason why Spark uses Java serializer by default is the overhead of registering all the custom classes. To register custom classes you can either specify them programmatically:

```
configuration.registerKryoClasses(Array(classOf[CustomClassOne],
        classOf[CustomClassTwo]))
```

Or you can set them in the `spark-defaults.conf` file:

```
spark.kryo.classesToRegister=org.x.CustomClassOne,org.x.CustomClassTwo
```

Kryo Registrators

It's important to know that during deserialization the registered classes must have the exact same ID as they had during serialization. When Kryo registers the classes it assigns them the next available integer. This means that you will have to specify the exact same order of the registered classes.

There is a workaround to this potential issue: In Spark, you can change the default way of registering classes in Kryo by writing your own registrator and setting it to the `spark.kryo.registrator`. Your custom registrator has to extend the KryoRegistrator and has to implement the `registerClasses(kryo Kryo)` method. In this method you could explicitly specify the class IDs to make the order in which you register classes unimportant:

```
kryo.register(classOf[CustomClassOne], 0)
kryo.register(classOf[CustomClassTwo], 1)
kryo.register(classOf[CustomClassThree], 2)
```

You can also take advantage of the fact that you can add your custom registrator to change the default serializers for your classes:

```
kryo.register(classOf[CustomClassOne], new CustomSerializerOne())
kryo.register(classOf[CustomClassTwo], new CustomSerializerTwo())
```

Spark Cache

Spark supports caching intermediary results in memory. When caching an RDD, Spark partitions will be stored in memory or on disk (depending on how it was requested) on the node that computed them. For future actions that are made on top of that dataset or on others derived from it, Spark won't re-compute it. Instead, Spark will return the data from the persisted partitions making future actions much faster.

To mark an RDD to be persisted, you call the `cache()` or `persist()` methods on it. The RDD is cached when you perform the first action on it. So in the example below, only the collect action will benefit from the pre-computed values:

```
myRdd.cache()
myRdd.count()
myRdd.collect()
```

We previously mentioned that there are two methods to let Spark know that the RDD has to be temporarily stored after being computed: `persist()` or `cache()`. They both store the computed RDD in memory by default. The difference between them is that `persist()` also provides an API for specifying the storage level for the case in which you want to change the default behavior. There are several ways of persisting an RDD:

- **Only in memory**—When using this type of storage level, Spark stores the RDD as an unserialized Java object in memory. If Spark estimates that not all the partitions will fit into memory, it will simply just not store all of them. If they are needed later on during the processing pipeline, they will be recomputed based on the RDD lineage.

  - Using this level of storage is useful when you frequently perform operations on a certain RDD or you require low-latency access.

  - However, there are also some drawbacks: You will use a larger amount of memory compared to the other storage levels, and also you might end up pressuring the garbage collector if you are caching a lot of small objects.

  - To cache your RDD using this storage level you can use one of the following methods:

    ```
    myRdd.cache()
    myRdd.persist()
    myRdd.persist(StorageLevel. MEMORY_ONLY)
    ```

- **Only in memory but serialized**—This time the RDDs are stored also only in memory but as Java serialized objects. This is more space efficient because the data will be more compact, so you will be able to cache more. The drawback of this storage level is that it is more CPU intensive because the objects are serialized and deserialized during each read/write. The serialized Java objects are stored as one byte array per partition. Which serializer you chose to be used while caching the RDDs is important (see the Serialization section).

  - Just as for the "memory only" storage level, if there are partitions that won't fit in memory they will be discarded and recomputed each time the RDD is used.

  - You can cache your RDD serialized in memory only using the following method:

    ```
    myRdd.persist(StorageLevel. MEMORY_ONLY_SER)
    ```

- **In memory and disk**—This storage level is similar with the "only in memory" one, meaning that Spark will try to cache the entire RDD in memory as an unserialized Java object, but this time if there are partitions that don't fit in memory, they will be spilled to disk. If those partitions are used latter on in other operations, they won't be recomputed but instead they will be read from disk. This storage level still uses a lot of memory and besides this, it also implies a load on the CPU and disk IO. You have to think which one is more expensive for your application: to write the partitions that don't fit in memory to disk and read them from there when needed, or to re-compute them each time you use them.

- Cache your RDD in memory and disk with the following method:

```
myRdd.persist(StorageLevel.MEMORY_AND_DISK)
```

- **In memory and disk serialized**—This storage level is similar as the one above; the only difference is that the data is stored serialized in memory. This time, more partitions from your RDD will fit in memory, because they are more compact, so there will be less to be written to disk. This option is more CPU intensive than its analogue one "in memory and disk."

  - The method to cache your RDD in memory and disk as serialized objects is:

```
myRdd.persist(StorageLevel.MEMORY_AND_DISK_SER)
```

- **Only on disk**—Using this option you will avoid storing anything in memory. The space used by your data is low, because the data is serialized. Because the entire dataset has to be serialized and deserialized and written and read from disk, the CPU load is high, and also there will be a disk I/O pressure. Example:

```
myRdd.persist(StorageLevel.DISK_ONLY)
```

- **Cache on two nodes**—All the above storage levels can be applied on two nodes of the cluster. Each partition from your RDD will be replicated in memory or on disk on two workers. API usage:

```
myRdd.persist(StorageLevel.MEMORY_ONLY_2)
myRdd.persist(StorageLevel.MEMORY_ONLY_SER_2)
myRdd.persist(StorageLevel.MEMORY_AND_DISK_2)
myRdd.persist(StorageLevel.MEMORY_AND_DISK_SER_2)
myRdd.persist(StorageLevel.DISK_ONLY_2)
```

- **Off heap**—In this case, the serialized RDD will be stored off heap in Tachyon. This option has a lot of benefits. The most important one is that you can share a pool of memory between executors and other applications, and the overhead brought by the garbage collector is reduced. Using the off heap persistence you avoid losing the in memory cache in case one of your executors crashes.

```
myRdd.persist(StorageLevel.OFF_HEAP)
```

If your Spark application tries to persist in memory more data than is supported, the least used partitions will be evicted from memory. However, the Spark cache is fault tolerant; it will re-compute all of the lost partitions so you don't have to worry that your application will crash. But you have to be careful what data you do cache and how much. When you cache your datasets with the intent to boost the performance of your application you might end up increasing the execution time. Put another way, if you try to cache a lot of unnecessary data, then the useful partition may be evicted, and then it will have to be recomputed before further actions can be executed.

If you are writing your application in Python, the RDDs will always be serialized regardless of whether you chose a serialized storage level or not.

Once your RDD is cached, you can see the information about it in the Spark UI, under the storage tab. You can view storage level, the number of cached partitions, and the cached fraction and its size for each storage layer (see Figure 3-9).

Storage						
RDDs						
RDD Name	Storage Level	Cached Partitions	Fraction Cached	Size in Memory	Size in ExternalBlockStore	Size on Disk
ParallelCollectionRDD	Memory Deserialized 1x Replicated	4	100%	160.0 B	0.0 B	0.0 B

Figure 3-9: The RDD cache information

In Spark Streaming, the data collected by Receivers is stored in memory using the MEMORY_AND_DISK_SER_2 storage level by default. Also if you persist an RDD generated by streaming computations, the default storage level will be MEMORY_ONLY_SER and not MEMORY_ONLY as in spark core. If your streaming application doesn't need to hold a large amount of data, you might consider giving up on serializing it, thereby avoiding the CPU overhead.

To remove an RDD from cache you could either wait until it will be evicted in the last recently used fashion, or, if you are sure you won't use it, call the method "unpersist" on top of your RDD.

```
myRdd.unpersist()
```

In Spark Streaming the RDDs generated by DStream transformations are also automatically evicted from the memory, but the behavior is a little different. Spark Streaming will keep in-memory data for as long as the window interval. The data older than the window interval is evicted from memory. You can change this conduct by setting the minimum duration that each DStream should remember its RDDs:

```
streamingContext.remember(duration)
```

To choose the right persistence level it's important to know your data and your hardware well, and how you intend to use them. Deciding between these levels is in fact deciding between memory usage and CPU. You have to be careful not to cache aimlessly. Be sure that the cost of added memory pressure or disk IO load is worth the savings of avoiding re-computation. If the space is something more important to your application than the CPU, then you might consider also compressing the serialized objects. You can enable this by setting the `spark .rdd.compress` property to true.

Spark SQL Cache

Just as in the case of caching frequently used RDDs, you can also cache tables on which you know you will perform a lot of queries. The Spark SQL cache mechanism is slightly different in that the cached tables are stored in memory in a columnar format. This is an important feature, because it won't go through the entire dataset during queries; only the required columns will be scanned, which leads to a huge performance boost.

   If your data is being saved in a columnar format, this also makes it possible for Spark SQL to automatically choose the best compression codec per column, fine-tuning it in order to minimize the memory usage and the garbage collection pressure.

   The following are some examples of how to cache a table:

```
dataFrame.cache()
sparkSqlContext.cacheTable("myTableName")
sparkSqlContext.sql("cache table myTableName")
```

   Another difference between the Spark cache and Spark SQL cache is that when you mark an RDD to be cached, it will actually get persisted after executing an action. It is easy to understand why: You have to compute the RDD in order to cache it. In Spark SQL, on the other hand, caching a table is easy. The table will be cached when you request it. This is the default option but you can change it:

```
sparkSqlContext.sql("cache lazy table myTableName")
```

To free the memory, you can manually remove a table from cache:

```
dataFrame.unpersist()
sparkSqlContext.uncacheTable("myTableName")
sparkSqlContext.sql("uncache table myTableName")
```

Memory Management

The main resources Spark needs are CPU and memory. We have already seen how CPUs together with partitions influence the parallelism level of our applications. Now we will focus on memory usage and the ways we can improve performance by tuning the memory. Next, we will describe situations when Spark uses the cluster's memory.

During the shuffle phases, Spark keeps in-memory intermediary results used for aggregations and co-groups. The amount of memory of the in-memory maps used for shuffling is limited by the value passed to the `spark.shuffle.memoryFraction` property only if the `spark.shuffle.spill` is set to true. If the data exceeds this limit, it will be spilled to disk. Each reducer creates a buffer in which it will fetch the output data of each map task. This buffer is kept in memory and has a fixed size per reducer, so unless you have a lot of memory, you should keep it small. The size of this buffer can be specified through the `spark.reducer.maxSizeInFlight`.

Spark also makes good use of memory when you cache the RDDs. The amount of memory used for persisting datasets is limited to a fraction of the overall Java heap. This limit is set through the `spark.storage.memoryFraction`.

Of course, Spark also uses memory when executing the user code, which might allocate memory for huge objects. The user code will take the rest of the heap after the one used for persistence and shuffling is allocated.

If you don't specify otherwise, by default, Spark will give 60 percent from the Java heap to persistence, 20 percent to shuffles, and its remaining 20 percent for executing the user code. You can fine-tune these percentages if you think they don't fit your use case.

Because Spark stores this large amount of data in-memory, it strongly depends on Java memory management and garbage collection. Knowing how to properly tune the GC improves performance.

Before we discuss how garbage collection influences Spark's application efficiency, we should first remember how garbage collection works in Java.

Garbage Collection

Based on how long an object's lifecycle is, it is stored either in the Young or Old generations in which the Java heap space is divided. Short-lived objects are stored in the Young generation while the long-lived ones are stored in the Old generation. The Young generation region is also divided into three sections: Eden and two Survivor regions.

When an object is first created, it will be written in Eden. When Eden fills up, a minor GC (garbage collection) is triggered. During this phase all of the alive objects from Eden and from SurvivorNo1 will be moved to SurvivorNo2, then the Survivors are swapped. When the alive objects from SurvivorNo2 are old enough or the space allocated for SurvivorNo2 is full, the objects are moved to the Old generation space. When the Old generation space is almost full, then a full GC is triggered. This is the moment when performance is highly impacted as the application threads are stopped while the objects in the Old generation are organized.

To measure the impact the GC has on your application you can edit the SPARK_JAVA_OPTS environment variable or you set the `spark.executor.extraJavaOptions` property in SparkConf by adding:

```
-verbose:gc -XX:+PrintGCDetails -XX:+PrintGCTimeStamps
```

The detailed garbage collector log can be inspected in the executor's log (on every worker node in the cluster). In this way we can track the entire GC activity. We can analyze when and why threads are paused, the average and maximum CPU time, the cleanup results, etc.

Based on these statistics we can fine-tune the GC. If we observe in the logs that the full garbage collection is called multiple times before the tasks finish, this means that there is not enough memory to run the tasks. Also if we observe in logs that the old generation is almost full, this means that we might use too much memory for caching. In both cases we should decrease the memory used for caching.

On the other hand, we might observe that there are a lot of minor GCs and not so many full ones. In this case it might help to allocate more space for Eden. You should scale up the space with 4/3 to take into account also the space dedicated to the survivors.

Garbage collection plays a very important role in Spark Streaming applications, because they require a low latency. Therefore long pauses generated by GC are unwanted. In this particular case, to keep the GC pauses constantly low, we recommend you use the concurrent mark-and-sweep GC on both driver and executors.

To summarize, if you observe that your application's performance is decreasing, you have to make sure that you are efficiently using the heap memory for caching. If you leave more heap space for the program's execution, garbage collection will be more efficient. On the other hand if you allocate too much heap space for caching and you don't take care how you use this space (where we excessively consume the memory) then you might end up with a large number of objects in the GC old generation, leading to a great performance loss. You can easily improve performance by explicitly cleaning the cached RDDs when you no longer need them.

Shared Variables

Spark has two types of shared variables: the broadcasted variables and the accumulators. They are designed to answer two common usage patterns: The former one is used to distribute large data across the cluster in order to be shared between tasks, while the latter one is used to aggregate information from the workers back to the driver. In the next few pages we will go through the significant details about how these shared variables work.

Before moving further you must understand how Spark deals with closures. A closure is a function, which has external references: It depends on variables declared outside it but in its scope. In the following example we define a closure that will raise a number to a power; the power is defined outside the declared function:

```
val power = 2
val raiseToPower =  (number : Double) => pow(number, power)
```

What about when you are executing closures in a distributed fashion across a cluster? First Spark computes the closure, then serializes it, and copies it within each task. Example:

```
import scala.math._
val myRdd = sc.parallelize(Array(1,2,3,4,5,6,7))
val power = 2
myRdd.foreach(pow(_,power))
```

In this example, the power variable is declared outside the function passed to the `foreach` method. This value will be copied with each task within the serialized closure.

Broadcast Variables

Following the previous example, let's try to imagine that instead of using a simple variable that stores the power on which to raise the elements from our array, we have a large dictionary that maps an integer ID to a sentence. We are using this dictionary to look up each integer from our integer Array. Here is an example:

```
val myRdd = sc.parallelize(Array(1,2,3,4,5,6,7))
val myDictionary = Map(1 -> "sentence1", 2 -> "sentence2", ..)
myRdd.foreach(value =>
    print(myDictionary.getOrElse(value, "Doesn't exist")))
```

The previous code will serialize the dictionary inside the enclosed closure and copied to each task. This means that if, for example, the RDD has 1,000 partitions spread across 100 nodes in a cluster, the dictionary will be copied 1,000 times, 10 times per node. If the dictionary is large, we can imagine what performance overhead it brings.

The broadcast variables are the solution for this type of performance issue. The broadcast variables are shared read-only values that are copied on each executor and cached in memory on every node. Spark copies these variables only once per machine and shares them between tasks instead of copying them within each task. This time, if we have an RDD with 1000 partitions on 100 nodes in the cluster, the dictionary will be copied only 100 times instead of 1,000 times.

The following code broadcasts the dictionary instead of shipping it within the closure on each task:

```
val myRdd = sc.parallelize(Array(1,2,3,4,5,6,7))
val myDictionary = Map(1 -> "sentence1", 2 -> "sentence2", ..)
val broadcastedDict = sc.broadcast(myDictionary)
myRdd.foreach(value => print(broadcastedDict.value
            .getOrElse( value, "Doesn't exist")))
```

Figure 3-10 exemplifies how the depending variables are copied whether you are broadcasting them, or not.

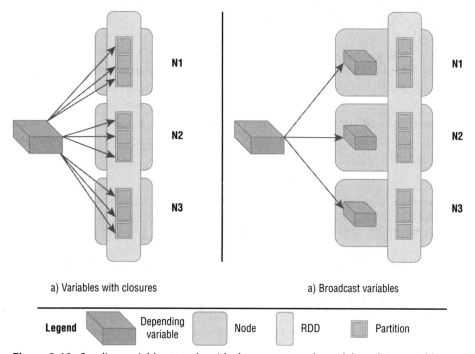

a) Variables with closures   a) Broadcast variables

Legend   Depending variable   Node   RDD   Partition

Figure 3-10: Sending variables to tasks with closures versus through broadcast variables

The broadcast variables are read-only in order to be consistent and fault tolerant. If they were otherwise, then, when a variable changes on one node, all of the other copies from the other machines will also have to be modified. To avoid these problems, Spark supports only read-only variables.

When you request that a variable be broadcasted, the Spark driver will write the data inside a local folder and into the block manager being identified with a block ID. When submitting a task, the transformation functions that use the broadcasted variables will be serialized alongside the metadata information about the broadcasted variable. This serialized information will be spread across the cluster.

When the task ends up on an executor and it is being deserialized, it will try to read the object that is described in the metadata. The first thing it will do here is to try to read the variable from the local blockManager to see if the cache already has a copy of that object. If no copy is found on the local executor, the data will be fetched from the driver.

The way data is fetched is important because it affects performance. Spark provides two different implementations of how data is broadcasted: The HTTP Broadcast and the Torrent Broadcast.

When you use the HTTP Broadcast, the data is fetched from the driver through a HTTP server that is running on the driver's side. As the driver sends the data to all the nodes in the cluster, there might be a network bottleneck. The Torrent Broadcast avoids this network bottleneck. The main idea behind it is that the data is split into smaller blocks, and once an executor fetches a set of blocks, it becomes a seeder.

You can set what type of broadcast implementation to use through the `spark` `.broadcast.factory` property. To adjust the size of the blocks used by the Torrent approach you have to set the `spark.broadcast.blockSize` to the desired value. You have to be careful with the value you choose here because too large of a value will decrease the parallelism and too small of a value will put a pressure on the blockManager.

```
val configuration = new SparkConf()
configuration.set("spark.broadcast.factory",
"org.apache.spark.broadcast.TorrentBroadcastFactory")
configuration.set("spark.broadcast.blockSize", "4m")
```

To summarize, the broadcast variables are an option you should consider when you have several tasks that have to access the same variable. This will boost the performance of your application.

Accumulators

Accumulators are another type of shared variable, which you can use for aggregating values from the worker nodes back to the driver. Let's imagine that we have a dataset and we want to count the entries that accomplish a certain condition:

```
val myRdd = sc.parallelize(Array(1,2,3,4,5,6,7))
var evenNumbersCount = 0
var unevenNumbersCount = 0
myRdd.foreach(element =>
        {if (element % 2 == 0) evenNumbersCount += 1
         else unevenNumbersCount +=1
        })
```

In the previous example, evenNumbersCount and the unevenNumbersCount will be serialized within the closure and sent to executors within each task. This means that each task will compute the even and uneven counters for the partition they manage, but the total counts from all the tasks won't be aggregated.

To solve this kind of problem we use the accumulators, which provide a mechanism to safely update a variable shared between all the executors. Their values are computed in parallel within each task, and then they are added on the driver side. This is why the operation applied on them has to be associative.

To make use of accumulators you have to change the previous example as follows:

```
val myRdd = sc.parallelize(Array(1,2,3,4,5,6,7))
val evenNumbersCount = sc.accumulator(0, "Even numbers")
var unevenNumbersCount = sc.accumulator(0, "Uneven numbers")
myRdd.foreach(element =>
        {if (element % 2 == 0) evenNumbersCount += 1
        else unevenNumbersCount +=1
        })
println(s" Even numbers ${ evenNumbersCount.value }")
println(s" Uneven numbers ${ unevenNumbersCount.value }")
```

When we create an accumulator we provide its initial value and optionally, a name. The tasks running on the cluster can update this value, but they can't read it. Only the driver is able to read the accumulator's value (evenNumbersCount.value).

If we provide names for our accumulators, we can spot them in the SparkUI, which allows us to troubleshoot our application (see Figure 3-11).

Duration	GC Time	Accumulators	Errors
0 ms		Uneven numbers: 1	
1 ms		Uneven numbers: 1 Even numbers: 1	
1 ms		Uneven numbers: 1 Even numbers: 1	
1 ms		Uneven numbers: 1 Even numbers: 1	

Figure 3-11: Accumulators in Spark UI

If you want a custom behavior for your accumulators, you can provide your own implementation of accumulators. You only have to extend the AccumulatorParam class and implement two methods: zero that provides the "zero value" for the type you are accumulating, and the `addInPlace` method to specify how to add two values.

For example, if you are processing some files and you want to accumulate the filenames that were processed with errors, you could implement your own accumulator in the following way:

```
object ErrorFilesAccum extends AccumulatorParam[String] {
  def zero(initialValue: String): String = {
    initialValue
  }
  def addInPlace(s1: String, s2: String): String = {
      s1+","+s2
  }
}
```

Then you can instantiate it and use:

```
val errorFilesAccum = sc.accumulator ("","ErrorFiles") (ErrorFilesAccum)
```

You can also have an accumulator that has as an input a certain type, but the result is of a different type. To have such an accumulator you have to provide your own accumulator behavior by implementing a more general interface called `Accumulable`.

The accumulators are very useful in troubleshooting. Possible scenarios include when you want to count the number of successful operations compared with the number of failed ones, or you want to count how many times a certain operation is being executed, or an issue that is relevant to the business case.

One aspect of accumulators that is important for you to know is that they should be computed only in actions—not in transformations. This is because of Spark's fault tolerance mechanism. Spark will automatically re-execute tasks if they fail or if they are too slow. If a node crashes while performing a transformation, the task will be launched on a different machine. The same thing happens if a task takes too long on a node. If some partitions are evicted from cache but they are needed in a computation, they will be recomputed based on RDD's lineage. So what we want to emphasize here is the fact that a certain function might be executed several times on the same partition of the dataset, depending on several events on the cluster leading to unreliable accumulator value.

Once you understand this behavior, you know that if you want a reliable value for your counters, regardless what happens on the cluster, you need to update the accumulators inside actions, and not transformations. For actions, Spark assures the fact that a task update over an accumulator is made only once. You don't have this guarantee when using transformations: The accumulator might be updated more than once inside a transformation.

Data Locality

Data locality is important to any distributed processing engine because it highly impacts the performance. Spark takes this into account by scheduling the task execution based on the distribution of the dataset across the cluster and, of course, based on the available resources.

If the code that processes a subset of a dataset is not in the same place that the data is located, then they have to be moved together. Obviously, it is faster to move the code to the data rather than moving the data to the code. This is also how Spark operates: It moves the serialized code to the workers where the data is placed.

If we were to define data locality then, we would say that it determines how close the code is that needs to be executed to the place where the data resides. Let's look at the various data locality levels:

- **PROCESS_LOCAL**—This is the best level as the data is located in the same JVM as the one within the code executes.

- **NODE_LOCAL**—The data is on the same worker, but it is not in the JVM. This implies a cost of moving the data between processes.

- **NO_PREF**—Data has no locality preference, and it can be accessed equally from any place.

- **RACK_LOCAL**—Data is located on a different server but within the same rack.

- **ANY**—The data is on a different server and not on the same rack.

These locality levels were ordered starting with the closest level and ending with the farthest one. Spark schedules the task execution so that it obtains the closest locality level. However, sometimes it has to give up on a close locality level in favor of a farther one because of resources reasons. In situations where the executors that are on the same machine as the data that has to be processed are busy and there are idle executors that are farther from the data, Spark waits for a certain amount of time for the executors to finish the work they are doing. If the executor doesn't become available, however, then a new task will be launched on one of the available nodes. This means that the data will be shipped to that node.

You can configure the amount of time for Spark to wait for an executor to become free for each individual data locality level, or for all of them together. Example:

```
val configuration = new SparkConf()
configuration.set("spark.locality.wait", "3s")
configuration.set("spark.locality.wait.node", "3s")
configuration.set("spark.locality.wait.process", "3s")
configuration.set("spark.locality.wait.rack", "3s")
```

Summary

In this chapter we have gone through some of the main factors that influence the performance of a Spark application. The purpose of this chapter was to raise awareness for how the coding decisions we make strongly influence the execution of our applications. To do that, we had to better understand Spark's fundamentals.

After grasping all of these tips on how to avoid performance bottlenecks, we will continue by learning more about security concepts in Spark.

Security

In this chapter, we will cover the security architecture of Spark. Hadoop eco-systems, including Spark, are operated in multi-tenant environments, which means that a cluster can be used by more than one user. Your company might have several departments that use Spark for their own purposes, since it can often be wasteful to construct a single cluster per department. Therefore, sharing one cluster is common in enterprise usage, because it saves time and money.

But there are a couple of issues to note here:

- **Data security**—Spark clusters store various types of data in your company. Some examples are user activity logs, purchase logs, and access logs. Some of them can be accessed by everyone, and of course some others can't be accessed by all. In order to protect your user data, you must manage the access control against the stored data.

- **Job security**—Even if data access is controlled by some mechanism, it is wasted if everyone can submit any type of job to the Spark cluster. Since each job can access data storage, it is also necessary to manage the authentication and ACL for submitting jobs. In addition to this, Spark jobs publish metrics through the Spark web UI and API. These must also be restricted.

- **Network security**—As often is the case in web applications, access can be controlled by host IP and port numbers. Otherwise, everyone can attack against a Spark cluster even from an external area. In order to manage a firewall to protect a Spark cluster, you must know every service that Spark provides such as web UI, REST API, and each port number.

▪ **Encryption**—Encryption is your last defense to avoid having your private data or network packets attacked and accessed.

Spark cannot yet provide all of the functionalities detailed in this list. But, Spark does provide sufficient security features and policies. In the following sections in this chapter we will explore Spark security. We will focus on the practical, rather than the theoretical, so we won't do a deep dive into the algorithmic detail of encryption and protocols. We hope you can configure your own secure cluster in your environment.

Architecture

The architecture of Spark security is very simple. Almost all of the security responsibilities are delegated to the SecurityManager in the Spark source code. This class is initiated by SparkContext (in detail, SparkEnv) to be accessed from all drivers, masters, and workers. So, the concrete implementation of your overall architecture can be checked by looking into SecurityManager.

Security Manager

Almost all of configurations will be passed to this class. The distributed workers can access the configuration from SecurityManager (see Figure 4-1).

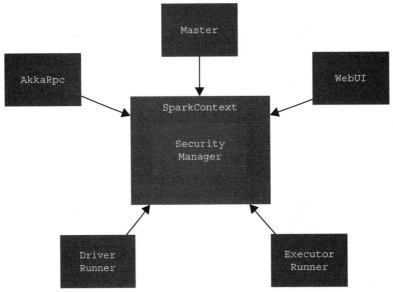

Figure 4-1: The SecurityManager is responsible for security configuration

As previously described, `SecurityManager` plays a role in keeping configurations about ACLs, authentications and filters. There are many types of configurations used for security on Spark. The detail of each configuration will be described here in the following sections. Let's get started by introducing how to set each property in your application.

Setup Configurations

There are three ways to set up Spark configurations:

Spark Properties, Dynamically Loading Spark Properties and Writing a static configuration file.

- **Spark Properties**—Through `SparkConf`, we can set up all types of configurations.

```
val conf = new SparkConf()
conf.set("spark.authenticate", "false")
// Create context object with your configuration
// This configuration will be reflected all
// components and executors used your job.
val sc = new SparkContext(new SparkConf())
```

  - This often requires modifying the code to change hard coded values. It is not an ideal case in development and trial cases. Spark provides the dynamic way to set arbitrary configurations.

  - AkkaRpc is used by a protocol layer using Akka. The others are Spark components.

- **Dynamically Loading Spark Properties**—Fundamentally, it is similar to Spark Properties, but you can set up through a command line interface such as `spark-shell` or `spark-submit`. It might be useful to change the configuration so you can keep running the same type of job. For example, when changing memory to test the effect of memory size to job performance you can set up the −`conf` option using the CLI.

```
$ ./bin/spark-shell —master <Spark Master URL>  \
          —conf spark.authenticate=false \
          —conf spark.authenticate.secret=secret
```

  - Of course you can use this option with `spark-submit` as well.

- **Writing a static configuration file**—In some cases, it is not necessary to change the configuration by each job. Rather, there are some configurations that should be shared widely by all jobs running on one cluster. In this type of case, it might be useful to write a configuration file. In addition to CLI tools such as `spark-shell` and `spark-submit`, the master server and slave servers of a Spark cluster read this file. By default, the `${SPARK_HOME}/conf/spark-defaults.conf` file is read by the Spark process. So, if you don't need to change the configuration every time, you can write it like this:

```
# Example:
    # spark.master                        spark://<Master URL>:7077
    # spark.eventLog.enabled              true
    # spark.eventLog.dir                  hdfs://<Name Node URL>:8021/ ⏎
directory
    # spark.serializer                    org.apache.spark.serializer. ⏎
KryoSerializer
    # spark.driver.memory                 5g
    # spark.executor.extraJavaOptions    -XX:+PrintGCDetails -Dkey=value ⏎
-Dnumbers="one two three"
```

You can see the template file (`$SPARK_HOME/conf/spark-defaults.conf`
`.template`) under the Spark directory. So from now on, if there is a time to set
some configurations for job or a whole Spark cluster, you can remember one
method to set these up.

ACL

The Access Control List (ACL) specifies which users or processes can access
which restricted resources. Each entry in the ACL expresses a user or process
and its permitted operation. Spark currently manages the ACL and attendant
authentication by using a *shared secret*. A shared secret is a token to be kept
secret among permitted users. It's like a password. So only a user who has this
shared secret can access restricted resources. In other words, you can submit
a job or see the process of the job with access. This shared secret mechanism
is a simple and basic authentication system that helps you secure your Spark
cluster. Next, we will explain how to configure the ACL feature in your Spark
cluster.

Configuration

There are three required configurations to enable ACL on a Spark cluster (see
Table 4-1).

Table 4-1: Required Configurations to Enable ACL on Spark

CONFIGURATION	DEFAULT
spark.authenticate	0
spark.authenticate.secret	None
spark.ui.view.acls	Empty

■ `spark.authenticate` is a parameter that specifies whether or not the
  authentication is complete. Since the default value is `false`, all users can

do anything on a Spark cluster without authentication. This parameter provides both job submission authentication and web UI authentication.

- `spark.authenticate.secret` specifies a shared secret to do authentication for a job submission. In order to run a job properly, you must match the shared secret between the token kept in the Spark cluster and the one passed with the job submission.

- `spark.ui.view.acls` is a comma-separated string that expresses the list of users who can access the web UI of the job. By default only the user who submitted the job can access the web UI for the submitted job.

Job Submission

In order to set the ACL for a job submission, it is necessary to set both `spark.authenticate` and `spark.authenticate.secret`. Let's confirm how it works with a stand-alone cluster on your environment. First, you can set up the configuration on your `spark-defaults.conf`. It might be nice to refer to the template file (`spark-defaults.conf.template`):

```
$ cp $SPARK_HOME/conf/spark-defaults.conf.template \
        $SPARK_HOME/conf/spark-defaults.conf
$ vim $SPARK_HOME/conf/spark-defaults.conf
$ cat $SPARK_HOME/conf/spark-defaults.conf
    # ...
    spark.authenticate                  true
    spark.authenticate.secret           mysecret
```

The properties are written and separated with white space characters. So, you can now launch the stand-alone mode cluster. There are utility scripts in the Spark directory to launch the master server and slave servers.

```
$ cd $SPARK_HOME
$ ./sbin/start-master.sh
```

You may find the master URL on the web UI. It is necessary to launch slaves, so let's check on `http://localhost:8080`. Next, launch the slave server. You can specify master server hostname from web UI as shown in Fig. 4-2

```
$ ./sbin/start-slave.sh \
        spark://SasakiKais-MacBook-Pro.local:7077
```

Now this standalone cluster has a secret token that you set in `spark-defaults.conf`. So, you can submit your job only when you have the same secret token. We can confirm that the submission succeeded or not using the CLI.

```
$ ./bin/spark-shell \
    —conf spark.authenticate.secret=mysecret \
    --master spark://SasakiKais-MacBook-Pro.local:7077
```

Figure 4-2: A Spark Master web UI snapshot

If a different secret is used, an exception will have occurred.

```
$ ./bin/spark-shell \
      —conf spark.authenticate.secret=wrongsecret \
     --master spark://SasakiKais-MacBook-Pro.local:7077
...
15/12/03 23:17:15 WARN AppClient$ClientEndpoint: Failed to connect to
master SasakiKais-MacBook-Pro.local:7077
java.lang.RuntimeException: java.lang.RuntimeException: javax.security ↵
.sasl.SaslException: DIGEST-MD5: digest response format violation. ↵
Mismatched response.
```

At last, you can construct the cluster where a user who knows the secret token can submit jobs, yet any users who don't know it can't. This is the simplest authentication system that can be used on Spark.

Web UI

Spark has a UI for each running job. When you submit a job, you can confirm the progress and configuration. Although there is useful data for checking the performance or for debugging the job, it is often inconvenient to publish this for all users. If there is no authentication, then all users can access the information below from the web UI:

- **Event timeline**—Visualization of the events induced by a job. You can see when each task is finished and check the bottleneck.

- **Stages information**—A Spark job is running accompanied by the unit called stage.

- **Storage information**—This is the data layer that a job uses.

- **Configuration values**—The configuration values for the job are listed. It is valuable for debugging and tuning.

- **Executors**—The information about executors on which the job is running.

All of the information should be secret in some cases, so we need to restrict access for the web UI. Spark uses the servlet filter to restrict and do authentication. This is set by the configuration in Table 4-2.

Table 4-2: Configuring the Spark Servlet Filter

CONFIGURATION	DEFAULT
spark.ui.filters	None
spark.ui.view.acls	None

spark.ui.filters is a comma-separated list of servlet filter classes. This class must implement javax.servlet.Filter. It might be a trivial thing for those who are familiar with servlet functionality, but it isn't often documented. We will introduce how to create a filter class for the Spark web UI. At this time, we will implement the filter that performs a basic authentication method that is not sufficiently secure. Although it is not fit for production to use directly, it might be helpful to explain a simple example here to get started.

A class that implements the javax.servlet.Filter interface must implement three methods listed next. You can see the detail of this interface here: http://docs.oracle.com/javaee/6/api/javax/servlet/Filter.html.

- void init(FilterConfig)
- void doFilter(ServletRequest, ServletResponse, FilterChain)
- void destroy()

The main point you need to pay attention to is of course the doFilter method. The servlet filter can do some filtering and authentication. So, if you want to do that for your job web UI, you have to write a filter class and add the class or JAR that includes the class. Here is the filter class that does basic authentication. You only need to add a user name and password to encode this data with a base64 algorithm. The request has to have a header: Authorization: Basic <Base64 encoded username and password>.

```
GET /jobs/index.html HTTP/1.1
    Host: example.spark.com
    Authorization: Basic c2FzYWtpa2FpOnBhc3N3b3JkCg==
```

The servlet filter code that realizes this functionality can be written like the next code snippet. The total code can be larger than the given space, therefore only paste the doFilter method here.

```
import com.sun.jersey.core.util.Base64;
import java.io.*;
import java.util.StringTokenizer;
```

```java
    import javax.servlet.*;
    import javax.servlet.http.*;
    import javax.servlet.Filter;
    import javax.servlet.FilterChain;
// ...
@Override
    public void doFilter(ServletRequest servletRequest,
                         ServletResponse servletResponse,
                         FilterChain filterChain) ↵
        throws IOException, ServletException {
        HttpServletRequest request ↵
          = (HttpServletRequest)servletRequest;
    HttpServletResponse response ↵
          = (HttpServletResponse)servletResponse;
    String authHeader = request.getHeader("Authorization");
    if (authHeader != null) {
        StringTokenizer st = new StringTokenizer(authHeader);
      if (st.hasMoreTokens()) {
            String basic = st.nextToken();
        if (basic.equalsIgnoreCase("Basic")) {
          try {
                String credentials ↵
                  = new String(Base64.decode(st.nextToken()), ↵
                        "UTF-8");
                int pos = credentials.indexOf(":");
                if (pos != -1) {
                  String username ↵
                    = credentials.substring(0, pos).trim();
                  String password ↵
                    = credentials.substring(pos + 1).trim();
                if (!username.equals("spark-user") ||
                      !password.equals("spark-password")) {
                    unauthorized(response, "Unauthorized:" +
                      this.getClass().getCanonicalName());
                  }
                filterChain.doFilter(servletRequest, ↵
                                    servletResponse);
              } else {
                  unauthorized(response, "Unauthorized:" +
                    this.getClass().getCanonicalName());
                }
          } catch (UnsupportedEncodingException e) {
                throw new Error("Coulndn't retrieve " +↵
                  authorization information", e);
            }
          }
      }
    } else {
        unauthorized(response, "Unauthorized:" +↵
          this.getClass().getCanonicalName());
    }
```

```
    }

    private void unauthorized(HttpServletResponse response, ↵
                              String message) throws IOException {
        response.setHeader("WWW-Authenticate", ↵
                           "Basic realm=\"Spark Realm\"");
    response.sendError(401, message);
        }
```

This is part of the implementation that uses the `BasicAuthFilter` class. All of the requested information is stored in `ServletRequest`, although it is necessary to cast this class to the `HttpServletRequest` class in order to manipulate it as an HTTP request. The authorization header can be restored using the `getHeader` method.

```
String authHeader = request.getHeader("Authorization");
```

Since the basic authentication username and password are encoded in base64, it is necessary to decode them. Spark writes Jersey as a dependency. So if you are developing the package for Spark, you may be able to use `com.sun.jersey.core .util.Base64` from your application code (Java 8 also has a built in Base64 decoder).

```
String credentials
      = new String(Base64
        .decode("c2FzYWtpa2FpOnBhc3N3b3JkCg=="), "UTF-8");
```

You can get the plain text username and password in `credentials`. They are separated with a colon. Next, split the string with a colon.

```
int pos = credentials.indexOf(":");
```

If it cannot find the ":", it returns `-1` as a definition. (`http://docs.oracle .com/javase/8/docs/api/java/lang/String.html#indexOf-int-`). Here is the main authentication code:

```
if (!username.equals("spark-user") ↵
               || !password.equals("spark-password")) {
        unauthorized(response, "Unauthorized:" + ↵
                  this.getClass().getCanonicalName());
        }
```

This code simply authorizes the user with a name "spark-user" and password "spark-password." It might be necessary to refer to a database that stores credential information for each user. But in order to make the problem simple, it requires hard-coded text. One note is that you must not use this type of code in a production environment. Credential information such as username and password must not be hard-coded in filter code. They have to be restored from some secret storage that is operated properly.

In this case, if either the username or password does not match to the stored credential information ("spark-user" and "spark-password"), it is unauthorized. You cannot then see the web UI provided from the application running on Spark.

Once you write filter code, you can include this class into your application JAR that will be submitted to the Spark cluster when running your application. When submitting an application you must set your filter in `spark.ui.filters`.

```
$ ./bin/spark-shell \
        —jars <The jar file including your application classes>\
        --conf spark.authenticate.secret=mysecret
        --master <The master of your Spark cluster>
        --conf spark.ui.filters=your.app.BasicAuthFilter
```

When you access your application web UI from your browser, you will be required to type the username and password. A popup will show if you are using Chrome (see Figure 4-3). If you type the username and password correctly, you will see the web UI of your application.

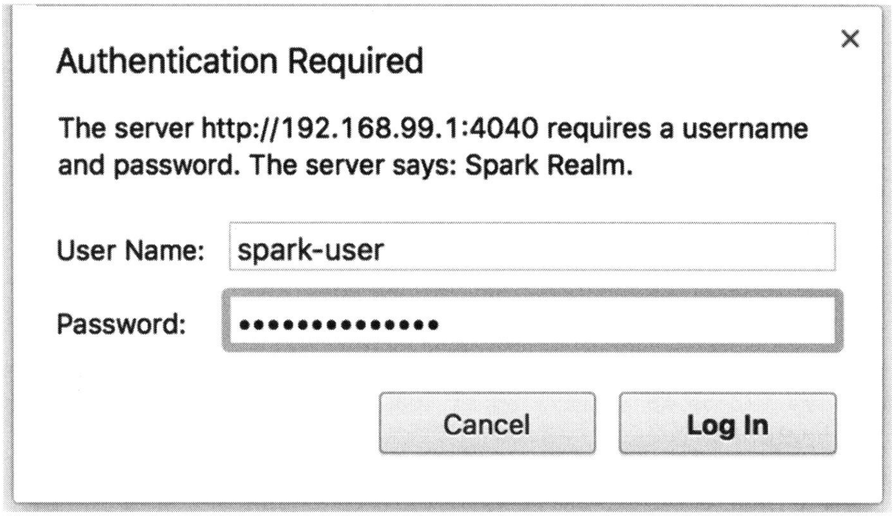

Figure 4-3: Popup showing username and password

This is a simple servlet filter. It might be sufficient in many cases for enterprise usage. But Spark has one more feature to do ACL for your web UI. As we explained previously, `spark.ui.view.acls` is used. This is a comma-separated list of users. The users listed here can only access the web UI. Note that the user who started the application can always access the web UI even though she is not listed here. The user name is restored by the method `HttpServletRequest#getRemoteUser()`. The method returns the user name who logged in your authentication system. As a trial, we will create a wrapper class that inherits `HttpServletRequestWrapper`. Now, let's implement the simple authentication system that realizes if the user name is set by a filter (in this case, assuming "spark-userA") and is contained in the user list (assuming "spark-userA", "spark-userB", "spark-userC"), then that user can log in as the username. So first let's implement the wrapper class called `UserListRequestWrapper`:

```
public class UserListRequestWrapper ↲
     extends HttpServletRequestWrapper {
   // Login user name
      String user;
   // Login database
      List<String> userList = null;
   // Original request wrapped this class
      HttpServletRequest request;
   public UserRoleRequestWrapper(String user, ↲
         List<String> userList, ↲
         HttpServletRequest originalRequest) {
            super(originalRequest);
            this.user = user;
            this.userList = userList;
            this.request = originalRequest;
      }
   @Override
         if (this.userList.contains(this.user)) {
            return this.user;
         }
         return null;
      }
}
```

This request class receives two parameters:

- `String user`—Specify the login username. In this code, this filter plays a role as an authentication system. The login username is set as "spark-userA" by filter. In reality, the login username should be set by an external authentication system such as Kerberos.

- `List<String> userList`—In order to simply implement an authentication system, the database that stores user credentials must be represented by `List<String>`. If a given user is contained in this list, the user will be authenticated.

This data is set by a filter. The implementation of the filter is similar to the `BasicAuthFilter`. You only write the `doFilter` method of the filter class called `UserListFilter`:

```
@Override
   public void doFilter(ServletRequest servletRequest, ↲
      ServletResponse servletResponse, ↲
```

```
                    FilterChain filterChain)
                    throws IOException, ServletException {
                    HttpServletRequest request ⏎
                            = (HttpServletRequest)servletRequest;
                    String user = "spark-userA";
                    List<String> userList ⏎
                            = Arrays.asList("spark-userA",
                                            "spark-userB",
                                            "spark-userC");
            // Passed the wrapper class that retains
                // the user list and login username.
                // The login user name authenticated here are
                // used by Spark application to decide show
                // web UI or should not.
            filterChain.doFilter(⏎
                    new UserRoleRequestWrapper(user, ⏎
                        userList, request), servletResponse);
        }
```

Through `UserListFilter`, all HTTP requests are converted to a wrapper request: `UserListRequestWrapper`. The login name is set to "spark-userA." We want to permit the access for the application from "spark-userA." So it is necessary to add "spark-userA" to `spark.ui.view.acls` when submitting your application.

```
$ ./bin/spark-shell \
        —jars <The jar file including your application classes>\
        --conf spark.authenticate.secret=mysecret \
        --master <The master of your Spark cluster> \
        --conf spark.ui.filters=your.app.UserListAuthFilter \
        --conf spark.ui.view.acls=spark-userA
```

When you access the web UI of this application, the login name is automatically set as "spark-userA," and this is permitted. Therefore, all information can be shown to you. If you don't set `spark.ui.view.acls`, you will see the warning in Figure 4-4 in your browser.

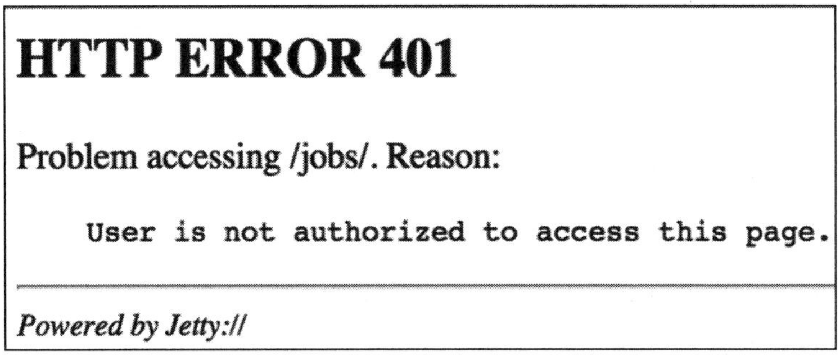

HTTP ERROR 401

Problem accessing /jobs/. Reason:

```
    User is not authorized to access this page.
```

Powered by Jetty://

Figure 4-4: The HTTP Error 401

So this means that the ACL against your application web UI is working. One thing to note is that the user who submitted the job can always access the web UI. And Spark has a configuration, `spark.admin.acls`, that specifies the admin user who can always access any resources provided from the web UI. This value is for specifying the administrators of your Spark cluster.

Network Security

Spark has a lot of different types of network usage. For example, there are interconnections between nodes in a cluster to transfer the shuffled data or HTTP connection between the client and worker to see the web UI provided by an application. Some environments require strict firewall settings in order to set the DMZ network or a separate global network and intra network. You need to know what service will be launched on which server and what number of ports will be used. In this section, we will introduce all of the possible connections around the Spark cluster. It might be helpful to write configurations for your firewall settings as shown in Table 4-3.

Table 4-3: Firewall Settings

CONFIGURATION	FROM	TO	DEFAULT PORT
spark.ui.port	Browser	Application	4040
spark.history.ui.port	Browser	History Server	18080
spark.driver.port	Executor	Driver	(random)
spark.executor.port	Driver	Executor	(random)
spark.fileserver.port	Executor	Driver	(random)
spark.broadcast.port	Executor	Driver	(random)
spark.replClassServer.port	Executor	Driver	(random)
spark.blockManager.port	Executor/Driver	Executor/Driver	(random)

These port numbers are used by any type of cluster management system (Standalone, YARN, or Mesos). Randomly chosen ports are used by interconnections inside the cluster. Usually you don't have to pay attention to them except for managing security issues. It is necessary, however, to know the number of ports in order to set up the firewall and so on. Since the ports listed in Table 4-3 are chosen randomly by Spark, you have to set the port number explicitly by configuration. You don't have any good way to systematically know the port number.

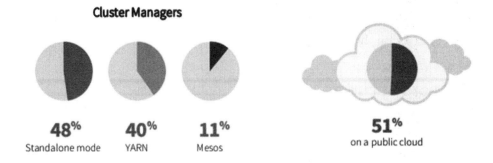

●databricks

Figure 4-5: Spark Summit EU 2015: Matei Zaharia keynote (`http://www.slideshare.net/databricks/spark-summit-eu-2015-matei-zaharia-keynote`)

If you run Spark on a standalone mode, there are some more ports you must pay attention to (see Table 4-4). Mainly they are web UI related, as you saw in previous sections. According to a *Databricks* report on the Spark Summit EU 2015, as shown in Figure 4-5. standalone mode cluster is most widely used. We will assume that most readers here will be using this cluster management mode.

Table 4-4: Standalone Ports

CONFIGURATION	FROM	TO	DEFAULT PORT
`spark.master.port.ui`	Browser	Standalone master	8080
`spark.worker.ui.port`	Browser	Standalone worker	8081
`SPARK_MASTER_PORT`	Driver/Standalone worker	Standalone master	7077
`SPARK_WORKER_PORT`	Standalone master	Standalone worker	(random)

If you have to restrict the access and connection based on IP and port numbers, this is the list in Table 4-4 that you should know.

Encryption

Currently almost all web applications such as Google, Yahoo, and Amazon support SSL/TLS connections between the client and the server. By using SSL/TLS you can encrypt the transferred data and send it safely without it being read by a malicious third party. Spark partially supports SSL/TLS connections. Currently, Akka-based connections and broadcasts and file server connections are supported. Internally, Spark uses a JSSE module for SSL/TLS communication. You may be familiar with JSSE, so you need to create a keystore and truststore to use SSL/TLS protocols with JSSE. The detail can be viewed on the Oracle official document (http://docs.oracle.com/javase/6/docs/technotes/guides/security/jsse/JSSERefGuide.html). In summary, the general process you need to do before setting SSL/TLS encrypted communication on Spark is as follows:

1. Create a private key for the server side.
2. Create a certificate signing request (CSR).
3. Get a signed certificate file from the certificate authority (CA).
4. Import a signed certificate file into trusted store.

Although official processes can be described like the list above, it might be a little tough to get a signed certificate from CA as a test or trial. So try to use a self-signed certificate to check the process of using SSL/TLS on a Spark cluster. Even if the signed process from CA is omitted, the overall process is the same for actual usage. Let's try to see what type of process and configurations are necessary here.

We will use the command line tool called keytool that is included in the JDK itself. You need to confirm that this tool is installed correctly and that the PATH is set toward the tool. For example, a local machine has a keytool under /usr/bin:

```
$ which keytool
/usr/bin/keytool
```

First, you have to generate a private key with the tool. Of course you can also use openssl or another SSL/TLS tool to create a private key. You can generate a private key using the -genkey option:

```
$ keytool -genkey \
            -alias ssltest \
            -keyalg RSA \
            -keysize 2048 \
            -keypass key_password \
            -storetype JKS \
            -keystore my_key_store \
            -storepass store_password
```

alias specifies the unique key name stored in this keystore. We will use the unique name from now on. Please don't forget the name. keyalg specifies the encryption algorithm used to generate a private key and public key pair. The size of the key pair is specified by keysize. The larger the key size, the safer the encryption becomes. The important points to remember are keystore, keypassword, and storepass. Keystore is a file that stores the generated private key, and keypass specifies the password used for using the private key. storepass is a password for keystore itself. After the command has succeeded, you can get a file named `my_key_store` that stores the private key just generated. You can generate a certificate file immediately because it is not necessary to be signed by the certificate authority this time.

```
$ keytool -export \
            -alias ssltest \
            -file my_cert.cer \
            -keystore my_key_store
```

`alias` specifies the same name to be used to generate the private key. This is used to specify the private keystored in the keystore created earlier: `my_key_store`. When you type this command, you will be required to type the password from the prompt. This must be the same password you set previously when creating the private key. If it succeeds, the file `my_cert.cer` will be created. This is a self-signed certificate file. One more step is necessary to use this certificate file on Spark. The last step is to import the certificate file into the keystore that can be used from JSSE:

```
$ keytool -import -v\
          -trustcacerts \
          -alias ssltest \
          -file my_cert.cer \
          -keyStore my_trust_store \
          -keypass store_password
```

If the `trustcacerts` is specified, other certifications in the default `cacerts` are considered to create a chain of trust. As you already know, `alias` is kept and used from earlier. With this command, the certificate file created previously is imported into a truststore whose name is specified by `keyStore`, and its password is also specified with the `keypass` option. They are also used in the Spark configuration. Please remember them. After all of these processes, you will have three files under your current directory, shown in Table 4-5.

Table 4-5: The keystore Files

KEY	DESCRIPTION
my_key_store	Private Key file
my_cert.cer	Certification file
my_trust_store	Truststore to be used to certify servers

Did you keep the password for the private key, keystore and truststore? They are required to set into the configuration file. The required configurations for

SSL/TLS connections on Spark are in Table 4-6, although many configurations need to be set. Spark currently supports SSL/TLS on Akka/file server communication. So, we can specify all configurations by the communication layer level except for `spark.ssl.enabled`. For example, if you set `spark.ssl.protocol=TLSv1.2`, this is applied to the Akka/file server based communications. On the other hand, if you set `spark.ssl.akka.protocol=TLSv1.2`, this value only applies to the Akka-based communication layer. This is for when you don't want to apply the same configuration for both communication methods (see Table 4-6).

Table 4-6: Configuration Methods

CONFIGURATION	DESCRIPTION
`spark.ssl.enabled`	Specifies whether SSL/TLS connections are enabled or not on your Spark cluster/application.
`spark.ssl.enabledAlgorithms`	A comma separated list of ciphers. They must be supported by JVM. You can find supported ciphers from here: (`https://blogs.oracle.com/java-platform-group/entry/diagnosing_tls_ssl_and_https`).
`spark.ssl.keyPassword`	Your private key password.
`spark.ssl.keyStore`	A path to the keystore file. This can be both absolute and relative from the directory the component is started.
`spark.ssl.keyStorePassword`	A password corresponding keystore file.
`spark.ssl.protocol`	A protocol specifying encryption communication. This must be supported by JVM. You can find supported protocols from here. (`https://blogs.oracle.com/java-platform-group/entry/diagnosing_tls_ssl_and_https`).
`spark.ssl.trustStore`	A path to the truststore file. This can be both absolute and relative from the directory the component is started.
`spark.ssl.trustStorePassword`	A password corresponding truststore file.

The example used can be similar to this:

```
spark.ssl.enabled               true
spark.ssl.enabledAlgorithms     TLS_RSA_WITH_AES_128_CBC_SHA,TLS_ ↵
RSA_WITH_AES_256_CBC_SHA
spark.ssl.protocol              TLSv1.2
```

```
spark.ssl.keyPassword                    key_password
spark.ssl.keyStore                       /path/to/my_key_store
spark.ssl.keyStorePassword               store_password
spark.ssl.trustStore                     /path/to/my_trust_store
spark.ssl.trustStorePassword             store_password
```

The keystore and truststore are used by every component of Spark, such as driver, master and worker. They should be distributed among the cluster. At this time, the single machine standalone mode cluster is used. Therefore, you can specify the same path and the same file as a keystore and a truststore.

After writing the configurations above in `spark-defaults.conf`, you can start Spark cluster.

```
$ ./sbin/start-master.sh
$ ./sbin/start-slave.sh <Master URL of Spark cluster>
```

You can now submit your job, because it is only used for internal communication inside the Spark cluster. Although you cannot see the effect of the SSL/TLS communication explicitly, a log can show how the SSL/TLS is working if the configuration was set correctly. In order to see the log, it is necessary to permit the DEBUG log to be written in a log file because the log of `SecurityManager` is set to DEBUG level. The output level can be changed by modifying the `log4j-defaults.properties` file.

```
log4j.rootCategory=INFO, console
↓
log4j.rootCategory=DEBUG, console
```

After restarting your Spark cluster you can see the log file under the `logs` directory.

Here is the master log file:

```
logs/spark-<Username>-org.apache.spark.deploy.master.Master-1-<Host ↵
name>.out
```

And here is the worker log file:

```
logs/spark-<Username>-org.apache.spark.deploy.worker.Worker-1-<Host ↵
name>.out
```

You can confirm that the SSL/TLS configuration is set correctly in the directory:

```
15/12/06 14:01:07 DEBUG SecurityManager: SSLConfiguration for file ↵
server: SSLOptions{enabled=true, keyStore=Some(/Users/sasakikai/ ↵
my_key_store), keyStorePassword=Some(xxx), trustStore=Some(/Users/ ↵
sasakikai/my_trust_store), trustStorePassword=Some(xxx), ↵
protocol=Some(TLSv1.2), enabledAlgorithms=Set(TLS_RSA_WITH_AES ↵
_128_CBC_SHA, TLS_RSA_WITH_AES_256_CBC_SHA)}
```

```
15/12/06 14:01:07 DEBUG SecurityManager: SSLConfiguration for Akka: ⏎
SSLOptions{enabled=true, keyStore=Some(/Users/sasakikai/my_key_ ⏎
store), keyStorePassword=Some(xxx), trustStore=Some(/Users/ ⏎
sasakikai/my_trust_store), trustStorePassword=Some(xxx), ⏎
protocol=Some(TLSv1.2), enabledAlgorithms=Set(TLS_RSA_WITH_AES ⏎
_128_CBC_SHA, TLS_RSA_WITH_AES_256_CBC_SHA)}
```

The configurations are set correctly as expected.

Event Logging

As described in the previous chapter, Spark has a feature called event logging to reconstruct the web UI. This logging data can be persisted in storage to be used later and to be decoded to show job information. In other words, these files keep the job information necessary to be shown in the web UI. It is necessary to restrict access to these files for the same reason why we restrict access toward the web UI of our applications. The file will be read by a history server later. So the file should be owned by the super user who is running that service, with group permission. The group permissions should also be available to the super user group in order to avoid unprivileged users removing or renaming a logging file unexpectedly.

Kerberos

Hadoop originally uses Kerberos (https://en.wikipedia.org/wiki/Kerberos_(protocol)) as its own authentication system, because it fits the characteristics of a distributed system. Kerberos passes a delegation token toward Hadoop when a user can successfully be authenticated. Each service running on Hadoop can check this delegation token to decide whether a user is authenticated or not. So other ecosystems such as YARN, HDFS and Hive support Kerberos. It is nice to know how to use Kerberos and how to write configurations because Spark depends on these systems. Since there are good resources for you to learn the details of Kerberos and how to integrate Hadoop ecosystems, we will not explain that in detail here. But keep in mind that Spark is also a distributed system such as HDFS or YARN. Therefore, the utilization of Kerberos can make a secure and high performance environment on Spark as well. Here are some resources:

- Hadoop in Secure Mode (https://hadoop.apache.org/docs/current/hadoop-project-dist/hadoop-common/SecureMode.html#Hadoop_in_Secure_Mode)
- Kerberos: The Network Authentication Protocol (http://web.mit.edu/kerberos/)

■ Configure Secure HDFS (`http://www.cloudera.com/content/www/en-us/documentation/archive/cdh/4-x/4-2-2/CDH4-Security-Guide/cdh4sg_topic_3_7.html`)

Apache Sentry

Spark and the other ecosystems on which Spark depends have different semantics of security. For example, HDFS files for ACL are managed by file permission, but Hive has more complicated abstraction such as tables, partitions and files. They don't necessarily match the ACL semantics of the filesystem: HDFS. In addition to this, Spark jobs can be submitted by anyone by default. You cannot currently enforce authentication to each job. So how can you integrate a trusted resource and an untrusted resource correctly?

Apache Sentry is a system for enforcing role based authorization to data and metadata that is stored in a Hadoop cluster. Sentry provides the functionality to control and enforce the privileges on stored data in the Hadoop cluster for users and applications. Sentry (see Figure 4-6) has been integrated with Hive, Metastore/HCatalog, Solr, Impala, and HDFS. Sentry adapted the pluggable architecture to integrate with a new platform. Although Spark is not supported by Sentry currently, it is just a matter of time before a plugin will be developed to support Spark.

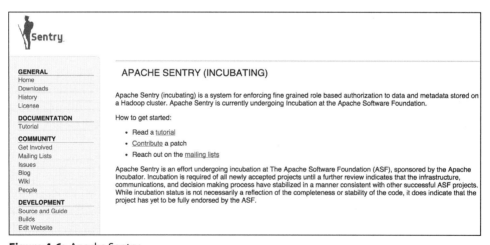

Figure 4-6: Apache Sentry

Summary

The security of multitenant environments is often a critical problem for enterprise usage. Although this problem is not restricted to Spark, Spark usually keeps and manipulates sensitive data for a business. Using various types of log data does not always protect personal information. But the combination of them often induces the outflow of personal information. The system to manipulate user data requires high level security protection mechanisms. This security becomes a critical problem in your company in terms of compliance with government regulations.

Regarding budget and money inside your company, security is also a critical problem. Authorization is necessary to realize the isolation of resources. In order to decide how much each user or department uses cluster resources, doing authorization correctly is required. The decision about the distribution of business resources such as a budget makes a significant effect on the investment toward future business. So in some way, security can also play a significant role to launch and progress new types of business in your company.

As you read, Spark provides the minimum functionality for constructing a secure data processing system. You can set ACLs data and jobs. Some level of encryption can be done with Spark. In many cases, we believe the security functionality that Spark currently provides is sufficient for usual enterprise usage. But some particular cases require a different kind of security policy that Spark cannot cover. You can submit a patch to resolve the issue to support your use case. This will be a nice contribution that others might want. All the processes can be done freely and openly, because Spark is developed by an open source community.

Fault Tolerance or Job Execution

It's common for applications to be initially developed as a proof-of-concept where job failures, extremely large datasets, and necessary service level agreements (SLAs) don't come into play. This is more so within Spark, given that most developers are starting out with the framework to accomplish such things like application migration, exploratory analytics, or testing machine learning ideas.

But, regardless of the initial application, there is a point in every developer's application lifecycle where they've scaled it to the point that it finally doesn't just "work out of the box." This can arise from Out Of Memory (OOM) exceptions, continuous job failures, or a crashing driver.

This chapter will focus solely on understanding those issues and how to build fault tolerance into your application so that it can be ready for the next stage of its lifecycle (i.e., production). Specifically, we'll explore the how and why of job scheduling, the concepts and configurations necessary for making your application fault tolerant, and finally we'll look at inherent hardware limitations and optimization techniques present in the later versions of Spark (v1.5 at the time of this writing).

Moreover, we won't be discounting all of the various components of Spark either. With the advent of the new DataFrame API, SparkSQL, and others, we need to be sure that fault tolerance and job execution can be sustained, whether using the core of Spark or any one of its various component projects.

As developers, the components of Spark are a tantalizing and beneficial piece that cannot be left out. From GraphX to MLlib, Spark's packages are strong components in their own right. Now, you might ask that if we're covering Spark components here, will we also be discussing the various popular packages from the `https://spark-packages.org` site. To that, the answer is no.

We will begin with laying the groundwork by first understanding the lifecycle of a Spark application. This will include key components of the Spark framework such as the driver and workers, the Spark master, and their communication patterns. Since you've already read and understand about the various scheduling frameworks for Spark from Chapter 2, we won't be covering much of their specifics here.

Next, we dive into the various methods of scheduling jobs for Spark to run in production environments. This includes various components and tools of core Linux operating systems as well as the ways Spark can be executed through its own tooling. We discuss briefly the various ways of maintaining Spark applications through the application itself, as well as when this can be a successful methodology.

Last, we will dive into the meat and understand the fault tolerance properties of Spark. One of the key differentiators here is that Spark, with its components included, makes up two separate areas of fault tolerance that are loosely related, those are: batch and streaming. We will cover both and discuss their similarities and differences when thinking about application fault tolerance.

In addition to stream and batch computation, we will cover how each of the components discussed previously maintain their fault tolerance and reliability, how Spark can be tuned to further achieve fault tolerance and the tradeoffs to those configurations, and finally dive into the Spark components and their specific tuning parameters.

Lifecycle of a Spark Job

Since the advent of distributed computing, the lifecycle of large applications has become a paramount piece of information for a developer to fully build out a successful product. This is no less of an issue when discussing a Spark application.

Before we dive too far into the lifecycle of a Spark application we first need to reiterate the various components constructing the Spark framework. This includes the Spark master, driver, and worker nodes (see Figure 5-1). Without these core components interoperating together, Spark would not be able to perform the tasks necessary.

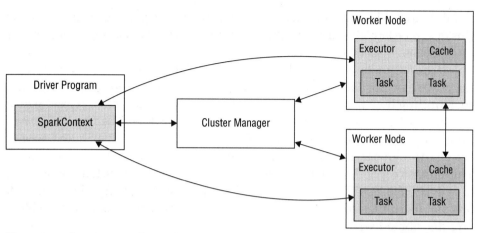

Figure 5-1: Components of a Spark application (This is from `http://spark.apache.org/docs/latest/cluster-overview.html`.)

Spark Master

Within Spark there is what is known as the Spark master. This is a server-side application that provides scheduling decisions to the rest of the framework. There is always only one master service unless explicitly stated otherwise for high availability, which we discuss more in later sections.

The master's primary role is to negotiate resources against the various resource managers as covered in Chapter 2. This is even done when running Spark locally as demonstrated with this code:

```
$ spark-submit --master local[8]
```

The Spark master, as stated above, is what performs the myriad of scheduling decisions that Spark needs to ensure each individual worker (discussed below) can be successful, even in failure scenarios. It is the primary control between the given application that you would want to execute and the underlying hardware that will perform the duty.

To set up the Spark master under high availability (HA) you also need to add another dependency into the mix, that of Apache ZooKeeper. Before we can go much further, let's take a brief foray into what ZooKeeper provides when discussing availability and fault tolerance.

Apache ZooKeeper

Apache ZooKeeper is a distributed, masterless coordination service. What does that really mean? It's assumed we're all on the same page with distributed, but with respect to a masterless service, it is one where there is no central point of coordination. Without a central point of coordination, each ZooKeeper node in a cluster can be launched and has the individual capability within the application to act as both a client and server.

Coordination, however, is the key to what ZooKeeper was made to do. In the advent of this latest wave of distributed systems, there was a large gap surrounding how to perform and execute various distributed services such as naming, locking, and synchronization. This gap was then filled by the Apache ZooKeeper application. Concretely, ZooKeeper performs distributed coordination through a quorum process such that no individual node is out of sync. This creates capabilities where developers can write distributed applications to leverage the ZooKeeper service for determining if a given individual node has the distributed lock, to determine where another node exists, or to block on a distributed write.

We won't be going much further into Apache ZooKeeper in this book, but when looking at taking a Spark application into production, ZooKeeper will most likely play a part. Therefore, if this is a new concept being brought up, it is recommended to pause here, read up on the documentation at `https://zookeeper.apache.org/`, and prepare a fault tolerant ZooKeeper setup.

Now that we have our distributed coordination setup, we can continue on to understand what we need to do with the Spark master service to ensure it is fault tolerant. With ZooKeeper available as a service, the Spark master can be brought up enabled to rely on that service to ensure that only a *single master* is in charge at any given time. This provides the ability for the current master to fail on any given node and any other master to become the leader. This happens through the election process within ZooKeeper, and, since the state of a given master is stored within ZooKeeper, the new master is passed the state of the previous, and continues where its predecessor left off.

Let's look at the configuration properties you need to set to enable this type of fault tolerance in your own application:

```
spark.deploy.recoveryMode  = "ZOOKEEPER"
spark.deploy.zookeeper.url = "127.0.0.1:2181,127.0.0.2:2181,127.0.0.3 ↵
:2181"
spark.deploy.zookeeper.dir = "/spark/master"
```

The above properties should be set within the `spark-env` file when submitting the application for execution under the SPARK_DAEMON_JAVA_OPTS property. Concretely, using the example values above, the single line you would want to put into your `spark-env` file would be as follows:

```
export SPARK_DAEMON_JAVA_OPTS="-Dspark.deploy.recoveryMode=ZOOKEEPER\
                            -Dspark.deploy.zookeeper.url=127.0.0.1: ↵
2181\
                            -Dspark.deploy.zookeeper.dir=/spark/ ↵
master"
```

Let's explore these properties starting with the recovery mode. To enable recovery through ZooKeeper you must set the mode to "ZOOKEEPER" (all capitals). Next is the ZooKeeper URL. At this point you should be familiar with it and understand that this is the host and port of each listening ZooKeeper instance within the given cluster. Last is an *optional* parameter, that of the ZooKeeper directory. This property defaults to /spark, but in the example above, to demonstrate, we've set it to /spark/master. It would be fine to omit this so long as there are no other developer-defined applications using the ZooKeeper cluster and, specifically, the /spark directory within.

Before we continue on with the Spark driver, let's pause and briefly mention the other resiliency option of the Spark master. As some might be aware, there *is* another paradigm in which the master can be recovered, but as we'll see in later sections, it not only is less stable, but it also requires additional external processes, which we want to minimize.

All that said, Spark does have a master resiliency option whereby it is a single instance of the master, and the necessary state to bring it back up resides in the local file system. All Spark workers register with the master as usual, and all necessary states for each worker are then tracked locally. When the master fails (or *if* the master fails), then you need to ensure there is an external process to spin up a new master service. This new master will then continue forward with the known worker state as tracked in the aforementioned local file system.

Now, this method of resiliency comes with a few large flaws. First and foremost is that the state is all tracked locally on a single machine. If, for any reason, that machine or its physical hard drive becomes unresponsive it is not a question of whether or not you can spin up a new Spark master, but how to access the local data that it had written. Second, as we mentioned previously, it requires the application developer to build in various components to handle the failure scenarios in hopes that it will be performed gracefully.

For all the above reasons, we *do not* recommend using the second option for Spark master fault tolerance. If you were to go the alternative route, we leave it as an exercise to the developer to understand the various necessary requirements that should be built to ensure proper fault tolerance.

Spark Driver

The Spark driver, unlike the Spark master, is the primary maintainer of state across the Spark application; however, like the master, it also makes some scheduling decisions. The key difference between the driver and the master is its primary task and how the *user* interacts with it.

When developing an application and creating a SparkContext, a context used to execute Spark commands, that context actually resides on the driver application. Therefore, whatever the SparkContext is responsible for, so too is the Spark driver as the maintainer of the context.

To fully understand the capabilities of the Spark drivers let's first understand the capabilities of the SparkContext. The context is the primary gateway into the Spark framework, and, among other things, it establishes a connection to the Spark master as well as handling the collection process for data. Building on the latter topic, when you run a method such as .collect on an RDD to realize the operations that have happened, that data then centralizes *on the driver application.*

This is a key concept when discussing the migration path from development to production because methods like .collect are used often without realizing the impact they have on the system. To expand on its severity let's build an example application that leverages a file on HDFS taking up 1TB of memory. If you were to merely read in the dataset, assuming there was enough memory to account for the entire file *across the cluster*, it is highly unlikely that there is that much memory on *the driver node alone* if you were to then execute a `.collect` command after the read.

All too often these commands will crash applications as their useful system load, or more concretely their data size, increases. This, in turn, is a common issue when first moving an application from development onto a production workload, say scaling the useful load from 10GB to 1TB, for example.

Another key issue to watch out for, depending on the underlying resource manager, is where the driver application is placed. For instance, when executing Spark in a standalone cluster the driver can run in one of two places. The first is the client machine where the application was submitted to the cluster. The second option is to place the driver on a worker node as if it were another process within the application.

Choosing which option is right is highly *hardware and use case dependent.* To solidify this point let's look at two examples:

1. There is an application that requires a join between two large datasets. This requires that all data be housed in memory for each file and for each row in each dataset to be known for the given join criteria. Assuming the datasets are 512GB per and each data node with the Spark cluster only has 256GB of memory, at 16 data nodes, both files will not fit on any *single* data node. In this instance it would be ideal to build out a client node with 2TB of memory, launch the driver application locally on the client, and execute the join on the client node.

2. There is a shared Spark cluster used by multiple individuals. They all reach the cluster through the client node, which only houses 64GB of memory. The cluster manages 50 data nodes each with 48 CPUs and 256GB of memory. All application workloads operate on single datasets no larger that 40GB at a time. In this case, given that the driver application, if used, would only need to store upwards of 40GB of data, it *could* fit onto any of the available data nodes. Additionally, because of the shared nature of the cluster, the client machine, where individuals launch their applications, is

resource constrained and shared between multiple users. For this example it would be wise to launch the driver application onto a node within the Spark cluster.

Now the above are two contrived examples with artificial memory constraints and calculations, but the premise of understanding the workload is what is key. The concept of understanding your application is peppered through this book and is paramount in driving success when moving the application into a production state.

So, how do you configure a given Spark application to leverage one or the other mode? Spark makes it quite simple, and for each mode, they've titled them client and cluster mode, respectively. In client mode the driver will be launched on the node that submitted the application. This is similar to the first example above. Conversely in cluster mode the driver application is launched within the cluster as demonstrated by the second example.

To launch an application in client mode you can manually specify it as follows:

```
$ bin/spark-submit --deploy-mode client <application-jar>
```

To launch an application in cluster mode is roughly equivalent as follows:

```
$ bin/spark-submit --deploy-mode cluster <application-jar>
```

It should be noted that, if no mode is specified with a cluster setup for Spark Standalone, the default deployment mode for the driver is client. Also, one thing we are not covering is how the other resource managers handle allocation of the Spark driver. Since this is covered in more detail in Chapter 2 we will not be covering it here.

Spark Worker

Spark workers are aptly named the workhorses of the Apache Spark framework. They are the services that get started on each node within a Spark cluster with the primary role of working with the Spark master to understand the work that needs to be completed. Each worker process is launched and, in turn, launches the Spark executor and, as we saw above, possibly driver processes based on the communication with the master.

Workers are, inherently, the most fault tolerant and resilient pieces of Apache Spark without needing any form of configuration. They were designed to withstand failures, interruptions, and errors with grace. This is one of the cornerstone developments that have made Spark such a strong framework for distributed computing.

When an individual worker is killed, for whatever reason, it will automatically be restarted by the master process. However, when a worker is brought down, so too are all of the executors and drivers running inside the worker.

Additionally, if a driver or executor crashes, but the worker remains active, the worker process will restart the individually failed portion of work.

Job Lifecycle

Now that we're familiar with the core components of Spark we can dive into the lifecycle of a typical Spark application. As you might expect the life of a Spark application is more in-depth than what is shown in Figure 5-1.

The job begins from the Spark driver application. This is the initial setup and launching of the job and, like we covered, handles the Spark context and all information thereof. The Spark master process, already being launched and running latent on the cluster, sits and waits for requests from a running driver. The driver, once connected to the master, will request a set of resources for its application. The master then will assess the workload and assign the tasks to a given set of worker applications that the master knows about. Each worker then launches a number of executor processes on its individual physical server to process the partitions of data it knows about. Each executor maintains its own thread pool and local storage for its operations. As the work is completed, the workers then respond to the master and/or the driver application to deliver data.

Let's take a look at a series of operations on an RDD as an example of thinking in the context of an application. Here is an example:

```
rdd.join(otherRdd)
    .groupBy(...)
    .filter(...)
```

In the above code, Spark will first turn the *logical plan* of operations on the RDD into a physical plan, which builds the directed acyclic graph (DAG). This DAG is then split into stages of tasks for each operation—here each operation is one of join, groupBy, or filter in this case. These stages are then submitted to the master to complete as they become ready. Any failed stages are then housed with the master, and it will recompute them as necessary.

Job Scheduling

On the journey to production there are many challenges to pass through. One of the more difficult hurdles, if never completed before or because of a new framework, is that of job scheduling.

In this section we are going to focus solely on how best to schedule Spark applications, what the developer can do to affect its ability to remain stable, and various external utilities to ease the burden. This will not, however, cover the various resource schedulers as seen in Chapter 2, but merely the interaction model between a given application and *any* resource manager.

Scheduling within an Application

Whether writing your application in Java, Scala, or Python, at the end of the day, Spark is merely a framework and library for that language to access a scalable compute grid. That said, you can easily mold, manipulate, or manage the framework to perform and schedule various workloads, all under the same framework and cluster.

As we've shown above, when developing a Spark application outside of the Spark shell you can own and maintain the SparkContext, therefore owning the scheduling and execution of the tasks. With that, let's start our journey there.

The SparkContext maintains all state and application logic when connected to the cluster, which we've covered already. What we haven't covered is the ability to control the SparkContext through multiple threads at the same time and the various abilities and constraints that come with it. As Uncle Ben always said, "With great power comes great responsibility."

Let's start with the abilities you get when executing the Spark context from multiple threads. First and foremost is the ability to execute another separate Spark pipeline—here we're defining pipeline as a series of operations on a dataset or RDD. This means that you could segregate or asynchronously parallelize work. Another power is that of asynchronous Spark jobs—here a job is a given Spark operation such as collect or save—submitted to the cluster all under the same context. This leads to the various properties of Spark's internal scheduler methods, which we will dive into in depth, shortly.

The constraints lie in the heart of memory management because the SparkContext handles all connection information, and data between the cluster and the driver, in turn, houses all necessary application information to maintain working stability. If or when the Spark context crashes or becomes corrupt, the application will then behave in myriad nondeterministic ways. This constraint realizes that developers should take additional care to understand what data they're moving, how the context is being utilized for their application, and how to mitigate production risk if the context were to crash unexpectedly.

As we discussed above, the SparkContext is owned by the driver application and, therefore, any scheduling of individual applications is done from the driver node. This is key when understanding resource limitations. Parallelization does not come without penalties, especially when discussing parallel data retrieval. Because each application is running from within the driver, any calls to retrieve data and collect it is then amplified. This is an oft-times forgotten issue when parallelizing the scheduling of an application.

Spark Schedulers

When dealing with the internal scheduling methodologies inside Spark there are two main types available. The first is that of the FIFO scheduler with FIFO meaning "first in, first out" with the alternative being the Fair Scheduler. This former type of scheduling is the default, and it's great when initially working with a new Spark application, but it's not ideal in most other use cases. The latter, modeled after the scheduler for Apache Hadoop under the same name, allows much more fine-grained control of resources.

Before we go too far into the scheduling let's first understand what a single Spark "job" is. In this context a Spark job is merely a single action called on an RDD such as a `groupByKey`. When that method gets called it is split into stages, such as map and reduce, with each stage needing a set of resources to complete their individual parallelized tasks.

With a FIFO scheduler you can submit multiple jobs from a single Spark context, and, for each job submitted, Spark will complete them in the order in which it was received. This means that if jobs at the head of the queue do not need to leverage the entire cluster's resources, then secondary stages can execute as well. If however, the first stage is large and consumes all available resources, that will leave nothing for any other job to leverage given the priority of the FIFO queue.

With the alternative of the Fair Scheduler we can defeat this problem. With this algorithm, tasks for each job are handed out in a round robin fashion—round robin being the process of giving the first task a single resource, then the next task a resource, and around, until all tasks receive a resource, which then repeats back at the first task until all resources are depleted. This allows the total amount of resources inside the cluster to be shared *equally* between all available jobs. Specifically this disables long running jobs from consuming all resources when other short-lived jobs could be completed alongside with a minimal set of resources. Those short running jobs then receive quick response times enabling additional use cases. Fair Scheduling is also highly preferred in a shared, multi-user environment. This is all enabled through the thread safety of the SparkContext object such that you can leverage it safely in a parallel manner.

The following example demonstrates how to configure the Fair Scheduler for any SparkContext:

```
val conf = new SparkConf()
conf.set("spark.scheduler.mode", "FAIR")
val sc = new SparkContext(conf)
```

Another capability of the Fair Scheduler is that of *scheduling pools*. These pools allow a user to define weights to each pool enabling further customization of how all of the resources in a given Spark cluster are allocated. This is especially useful for situations such as a "high-priority" queue allowing shorter jobs to finish quickly or to allow queues for multiple users.

When setting up the Fair Scheduler, each job afterward will move into the *default* pool. To enable separate pools, you merely need to add a local property into the Spark context used within that given thread. This thread will then use the given specified pool for all jobs *until reset*. Below is an example of how to set and unset a pool for a given Spark context labeled as `sc`.

```
// setting a pool
sc.setLocalProperty("spark.scheduler.pool", "<pool-name>")

...

<work for the given pool here>

...

// unsetting the pool
sc.setLocalProperty("spark.scheduler.pool", null)
```

By default, each pool under the Fair Scheduler will receive an equal weight, and, within each pool, FIFO ordering will take over.

To enable the full gamut of scheduling properties for a production workload, Spark enables all of these to be set *a priori* through an XML configuration file. Each pool receives a name, a scheduling mode, a weight, and a minimum share amount.

Weights, when configured, all start with a default value of one. This means that each pool receives an equal number of resources within the cluster. If, however, a specific pool has a weight of two, then it would receive *twice* the number of resources as every other pool. This is not a set number, but merely a ratio to weight each pool, hence the name.

The minimum share, tied to the weight, is the ability to set a minimum number of shares, as a number of CPU cores that a pool should have. The Fair Scheduler then attempts to fulfill all minimum shares first before distributing additional resources based on weight. This ensures a minimum set of shares to a given pool at all times *if resources allow*. By default, or without specifying, each pool will have a minimum share of zero.

Let's now look at an example of what this XML configuration file looks like:

```
<?xml version="1.0"?>
<allocations>
  <!-- high priority queue -->
  <pool name="high-priority">
    <schedulingMode>FAIR</schedulingMode>
    <weight>4</weight>
    <minShare>64</minShare>
  </pool>

  <!-- medium priority queue -->
  <pool name="medium-priority">
    <schedulingMode>FAIR</schedulingMode>
    <weight>2</weight>
    <minShare>16</minShare>
  </pool>
```

```
  <!-- low priority queue -->
  <pool name="low-priority">
    <schedulingMode>FIFO</schedulingMode>
  </pool>
</allocations>
```

What we've defined are three pools, each with their own scheduling mode, weight, and number of minimum shares. Additionally, Spark provides an example with its codebase at https://github.com/apache/spark/blob/master/conf/fairscheduler.xml.template.

With the configuration created it is simple to then enable it through code with the following line:

```
val conf = new SparkConf()
conf.set("spark.scheduler.allocation.file", "/path/to/file")
```

With the above examples we created three pools labeled "high-priority," "medium-priority," and "low-priority" with various weights, and then enabled that through a line of code. From here, with each Spark context, we can then leverage the pools based on their assignment. The key difference between a configuration-based scheduling system and one created through code is that each pool name is now defined in an external file. Those same pools must, however, be referenced with the same names for the jobs to make it into the given pool. Referencing the above example we can enable the given pool as follows:

```
// assuming the Spark Context is 'sc'
sc.setLocalProperty("spark.scheduler.pool", "high-priority")
...
<work for the high priority pool>
...
sc.setLocalProperty("spark.scheduler.pool", "low-priority")
...
<work for the low priority pool>
...
// reset the pool back to the default
sc.setLocalProperty("spark.scheduler.pool", null)
```

Example Scenarios

We've discussed a large degree of technical concepts, and it only benefits you to understand how to take those concepts and leverage them inside your application. With that, we wanted to provide an example application with emphasis on scheduling decisions as well as provide some code, and pseudo-code, to demonstrate the principles. This example is meant to reflect real world scenarios, albeit fictional, and provide a basis on how to scope various applications.

Our scenario is one in which there is a time-critical machine learning application. The model for this application must be retrained every 10 minutes and redeployed. It leverages an ensemble model technique, roughly meaning that the end model is built on a culmination of a few models. Understanding some general parallelism concepts, we realize that because this is an ensemble model, we can train each sub-model independently of each other. This will provide a clear speed enhancement from the sequential model training that could be done.

So how do you accomplish this task? Let's take a look at the general steps *before* we implement parallel scheduling:

```scala
import org.apache.spark.{SparkConf, SparkContext}
import org.apache.spark.ml.classification.LogisticRegression
import org.apache.spark.mllib.linalg.{Vector, Vectors}
import org.apache.spark.sql.Row
import org.apache.spark.sql.SQLContext

val conf = new SparkConf()
val sc = new SparkContext(conf)
val sqlContext = new SQLContext(sc)

val train1 = sqlContext.createDataFrame(Seq(
    (1.0, Vectors.dense(0.4, 4.3, -3.4)),
    (1.0, Vectors.dense(1.2, 9.8, -9.5)),
    (0.0, Vectors.dense(-0.1, 12.4, -2.3)),
    (0.0, Vectors.dense(-1.9, 8.7, -4.6))
)).toDF("label", "features")

val train2 = sqlContext.createDataFrame(Seq(
    (0.0, Vectors.dense(0.3, 4.5, 10.1)),
    (1.0, Vectors.dense(3.2, 0.0, -6.3)),
    (1.0, Vectors.dense(0.2, -8.6, 5.4)),
    (1.0, Vectors.dense(0.1, 6.1, -4.5))
)).toDF("label", "features")

val test = sqlContext.createDataFrame(Seq(
    (0.0, Vectors.dense(-0.2, 9.3, 0.9)),
    (1.0, Vectors.dense(1.1, 6.6, -0.4)),
    (1.0, Vectors.dense(3.8, 12.7, 2.0))
)).toDF("label", "features")

val lr = new LogisticRegression()

val model1 = lr.fit(train1)
val model2 = lr.fit(train2)

model1.transform(test)
    .select("features", "label", "probability", "prediction")
    .collect()
    .foreach { case Row(features: Vector, label: Double, prob: Vector, ⌐
```

```
prediction: Double) =>
    println(s"Features: $features, Label: $label => Probability: ↵
$prob, Prediction: $prediction")
  }


model2.transform(test)
   .select("features", "label", "probability", "prediction")
   .collect()
   .foreach { case Row(features: Vector, label: Double, prob: ↵
Vector, prediction: Double) =>
      println(s"Features: $features, Label: $label => Probability: ↵
$prob, Prediction: $prediction")
   }
```

Let's take the same example and apply the technique of parallel scheduling within a Spark application. Here we will leverage the SparkContext under multiple threads and call them asynchronously to train each model *simultaneously*:

```
import org.apache.spark.{SparkConf, SparkContext}
import org.apache.spark.ml.classification.LogisticRegression
import org.apache.spark.mllib.linalg.{Vector, Vectors}
import org.apache.spark.sql.Row
import org.apache.spark.sql.SQLContext

val conf = new SparkConf()
val sc = new SparkContext(conf)
val sqlContext = new SQLContext(sc)
val lr = new LogisticRegression()

val test = sqlContext.createDataFrame(Seq(
   (0.0, Vectors.dense(-0.2, 9.3, 0.9)),
   (1.0, Vectors.dense(1.1, 6.6, -0.4)),
   (1.0, Vectors.dense(3.8, 12.7, 2.0))
)).toDF("label", "features")

val modelExec1 = new Thread(new Runnable {
   def run() {
     val train = sqlContext.createDataFrame(Seq(
        (1.0, Vectors.dense(0.4, 4.3, -3.4)),
        (1.0, Vectors.dense(1.2, 9.8, -9.5)),
        (0.0, Vectors.dense(-0.1, 12.4, -2.3)),
        (0.0, Vectors.dense(-1.9, 8.7, -4.6))
     )).toDF("label", "features")

     val model = lr.fit(train)

     model.transform(test)
        .select("features", "label", "probability", "prediction")
        .collect()
        .foreach { case Row(features: Vector, label: Double, prob: ↵
Vector, prediction: Double) =>
```

```
          println(s"Features: $features, Label: $label => Probability: ⏎
$prob, Prediction: $prediction")
      }
    }
})

val modelExec2 = new Thread(new Runnable {
    def run() {
      ...
      val train = sqlContext.createDataFrame(...)

      val model = lr.fit(train)

      model.transform(test)...
    }
})

modelExec1.start()
modelExec2.start()
```

With the above example we can see how to leverage primitive synchronization techniques to further parallelize the application and greatly increase speeds. This is primarily caused by the nonblocking nature of the .start method from a Runnable object calling a new thread to perform the work we've assigned to it.

Another example could involve the development of a recommender system leveraging a 100TB dataset over a modest cluster of ten nodes, each with 64GB of memory and 12 CPUs. The added constraint is that the cluster cannot be resized or added to due to current budgetary constraints. In the current application the system continues to fail because it cannot house the gross corpus of data necessary to train the recommender across all of the data nodes.

So, how can scheduling fix this problem? Since time is not a constraint in this example we can segregate the dataset and build recommendations through a slower process of incrementally building recommendations for subsets of the overall data population. It is left as an exercise to the reader for the implementation.

To create success from the above scenario you should have demonstrated the usage of *multiple synchronous* calls to the SparkContext object. This allows you to incrementally execute Spark applications and manage each subapplication in turn while letting the driver application maintain the intermediate state between each execution.

In both scenarios the key points are about maintaining proper resource utilization by adding multiple synchronous or asynchronous calls to the SparkContext object and leveraging threading. Determining which is right for a given application is completely dependent on the resource allocation of the cluster that will be used as well as the requirements of success.

In the linear regression modeling scenario it was more dependent on the requirements for success having the model trained within 10 minutes and redeployed. This certainly created a need to scope hardware appropriately, but was bound to the aforementioned success criteria. In the latter case it was bound more on hardware *constraints* rather than the requirement of success. Success was merely to finish the job, but it required intimate utilization of the driver and scheduling to ensure that criteria could be met.

Scheduling with External Utilities

Often when taking an application into production there comes with it a large swathe of external utilities developed to ensure that the service is up, active, and in a healthy state. This is no different with a Spark application.

Spark comes with many great command line utilities and options, but at some point, those options will only go so far and do not cover the gamut of what is necessary for a production application.

Linux Utilities

There are quite a few Linux-based utilities out there specifically created to keep your application alive. There are a few that stand out more than others, and we'll cover the most common that have shown strong capability in production environments.

First is the trusted cron utility. This tool has been around since Version 7 Unix and has played a large role in the scheduling of tasks since it's inception. It has gone through much iteration, although it is still widely used and performs well under normal circumstances. It maintains a file labeled `~/.crontab` in the user's home directory where, through a domain specific language, you can configure commands to execute at given periods of time. An example of a line in a "cron" script is as follows:

```
$ cat ~/.crontab

00,30 * * * 1-5 /path/to/executable/script1.sh
15 08 06 04 * /path/to/executable/script2.sh
```

In the above we're running two separate examples. In the first example the script, aptly named script1.sh, is executed every 0th and 30th minute of every hour of every day of every month on weekdays (i.e., Monday through Friday). The latter example will execute script2.sh on the 15th minute at 8 a.m. on the 6th day of the fourth month (April). What is shown above is a good example of the simple usage of cron, but does not nearly go into detail. If this is of interest please check out the cron manual page at `http://linux.die.net/man/1/crontab`.

One place that this starts to show when looking at issues with cron, and why other systems that we'll discuss below were created, is because cron does not have any concept of tiered job execution—the concept of executing some job after a given job has finished, possibly with a given return code. It also creates the issue of *hotspotting*—a concept whereby multiple jobs will execute at the same given moment thus creating a large influx of resource utilization for a given node.

Airbnb has since created a modified version of cron titled Chronos, which is a modified version of cron atop the Mesos resource scheduler. It was open sourced in March 2013 and is a great alternative to the traditional cron command for any Spark application leveraging Mesos. Some of the key features that differentiate Chronos from cron are as follows:

- **Allows a developer to schedule jobs using the ISO8601 standard rather than the self-defined cron language**—The ISO8601 standard specifically allows for repeated interval notation, which allows for repeating a job a set number of times and optionally, at set intervals.

- **Creates the concept of a job hierarchy**—Chronos can trigger downstream jobs once their upstream, dependent, parent jobs are completed.

- **Supports arbitrarily long dependency chains**—When developing and decomposing a series of jobs that need to be chained together Chronos ensures that the dependency chain can always be fulfilled.

Another great utility out there that works for both Linux and Windows is a Python program called Supervisord (read more at `http://supervisord .org/`). This scheduler specializes in bringing back up failed applications after they've failed. While this sounds very useful for various portions of Spark this is actually only applicable to the launching of any given Spark job.

Where Supervisord comes in very handy is the relaunching of a given Spark application based on its exit code. While not perfect, this can provide another level of guarantee that the application will do everything within its power to run to completion. Supervisord has the specialty of now allowing the developer to worry less about external (typically operating system) anomalies and concentrate more on feature addition of the core codebase. Apache ZooKeeper actually recommends that all its services be started through a Supervisord monitor.

While this is not an extensive list of external scheduling capabilities, it provides a launching ground for a developer to begin exploring what their needs are for the given application. More often than not the scheduling dependencies that need to be added to the system are strongly tied to the business and technology requirements of the application being developed. This section was not meant to be an exhaustive list, but a capabilities introduction and overview to provide the scoping for understanding what work might need to be done with the application at hand.

Fault Tolerance

Once a basic application has been built on the Spark framework it needs to survive the migration into production. This lifecycle necessitates a single core value, that being fault tolerance.

What is fault tolerance exactly? It is the culmination of the following concepts—reliability, durability, and availability—that an application needs to ensure it meets or exceeds the demands its customers place on it in a real world environment. These customers could be human users or other machines pushing and pulling content from the service.

To simplify this idea, fault tolerance can be viewed as an application's ability to be *stable to external interactions*. We say "external" in this sense because, even if your application doesn't work internally for some reason (for example internal auditing or reporting features), as long as the customer or consumer of the application does not know or see a problem, then the downstream system would consider it a *stable system*.

Internal and External Fault Tolerance

The concepts of *internal* and *external* are relatively viewed as the same thing, but it's important to have a better grasp on their independent meaning. When putting any application into production it is good to have a general understanding of its *internal* and *external* fault tolerance needs. This is not to be confused with a service level agreement, as we'll discuss in the next section.

Why do you want to understand both the *internal* and *external* fault tolerance needs of an application? This is to help scope and provide a clear roadmap of the application's development. To understand fully let's dive into what both "internal" and "external" mean.

Let's begin with *internal* fault tolerance because this is predominantly what is seen and understood. When developing an application you assume that all features must work flawlessly. This includes all features the application developer knows about, the features that the customer will see, and the "back end" features that are only there to support other capabilities (such as log aggregation, auditing, or write-ahead logs).

When a feature doesn't work it affects the stability of the system *from the developer's perspective*. Concretely if *any* feature were not working as expected the fault tolerance of the system would be artificially lowered. This is predominantly based on a developer perspective whereby they view the system as a series of interconnected pieces. This is analogous to the blueprints for an engine of a car.

This leads to the concept of *internal fault tolerance*, whereby there is a measurement of the system (either quantitative or qualitative) from the viewpoint of the system as a series of interconnected parts that denotes the system's overall fault tolerance to both internal and external interactions.

Let's contrast that with the notion of *external* fault tolerance. The major differentiation here is in the *perspective of the system*. Before we discussed the perspective of understanding every component of the system, but as with a customer's point of view, what if you saw the system as a black box or oracle that merely provided outputs to your inputs?

In this latter case the system's fault tolerance can be defined simply as the percentage of correct outputs for given inputs over time. We can write this as follows where x is the input, f(x) is the given output, y is the *expected* output, and t is some measurement of time:

$$\frac{\sum_0^t (f(x) = y)}{t}$$

From the formula above we are assuming that the equivalence of f(x) and y will either produce a 1 or 0 depending on whether the output matched the expected value or not respectively. We can then divide by t, assuming t is equal to the number of inputs, to receive our correctness percentage for the system.

The key here, again, is the perspective with which the system is measured. *External fault tolerance* is explicitly a measurement of the system as black box and *only* takes into account the customers (again, humans or machines) that leverage the application.

Understanding both *internal* and *external* fault tolerance will help greatly when moving to production in understanding the various ways you can measure a system, how to scope the system as it moves through the production lifecycle, and finally how the system is perceived to current (and future) customers.

Service Level Agreements (SLAs)

Before we can discuss fault tolerance within an application we first need to understand the metric with which fault tolerance is measured, and that is through what is known as a service level agreement or SLA.

A service level agreement, formally, is a contract between two parties that determines the service level, or the amount of time it's available to a consumer/customer, for a given application. This, historically, has been seen with large-scale applications and, more recently, with cloud applications. For instance, if Gmail were to go down often then it would have a lower SLA and, therefore, if people couldn't access their email, gmail would lose their customer base. The same concept can be applied to the Amazon website. At times when there is a large customer draw on the system (i.e., when many individuals are navigating to http://www.amazon.com) such as Black Friday or Cyber Monday, it is critical for that system to be "in service." If the website were "out of service" then Amazon as a company would lose money because it couldn't serve its content to its customers.

These examples lie at the heart of the service level agreement that needs to be known, or discovered, when taking a Spark application into production. This is typically a larger question than the initial development of the application and, on most occasions, requires more parties to get involved (product owners, managers, engineering leads, etc.) to determine the SLA of the application.

The reason this becomes such a large issue and one that many focus on, although it is often forgotten, is because the service level agreement is a direct correlation to the amount of risk a business wants to mitigate. For instance, if the Spark application a developer wrote were to go into production serving dynamic ad content to consumers, then its uptime, or SLA, would determine the effectiveness of the application. Or, in other terms, the SLA would define the risk associated with that application *not* being in service.

For all these reasons when someone decides to take their application, be it Spark or otherwise, into a production environment, the service level agreement must be discussed and understood because it *will* affect nearly every aspect of the application. You need to factor in the labor costs it's going to take to raise the SLA from "the system must be on 99% of the time" to "the system must be on 99.999% of the time" as well as how that will affect the design decisions that have been instrumented already to get it as far as it has.

No one wants to rewrite code so, to mitigate that as best as possible, it is always a good idea to have an understanding of the service level agreement, be that between your company and the customer, your team and your company, or otherwise, at the earliest stages possible from the inception of the project. This will help scope and regulate the features of the project as it moves forward.

Resilient Distributed Datasets (RDDs)

Resilient distributed datasets (referred to as RDDs) are the lifeblood of Spark. We assume if whomever is reading this has done anything with Spark they've already encountered the RDD because these are the literal building blocks to any Spark application.

But what is an RDD exactly and what makes it resilient? This is actually the more fundamental question, and the research that created the RDD was the actual precursor to Spark as a compute framework. Formally, from the seminal paper of Spark (`spark.apache.org`), an RDD is:

... a read-only, partitioned collection of records.

So RDDs are read-only and partitioned. Does this define resilience? Going another step deeper we can see that one of the key features to an RDD is its ability to track lineage. Because an RDD is only *realized* on certain commands it needs to track the lineage of commands placed upon it to retrace in the case of an error. An example of a lineage would be the following code:

```
scala> val rdd = sc.textFile("<some-text-file>")
rdd: org.apache.spark.rdd.RDD[String] = MapPartitionsRDD[1] at textFile ⏎
at <console>:21

scala> rdd.toDebugString
res0: String =
(2) MapPartitionsRDD[1] at textFile at <console>:21 []
 |   spark-join.spark HadoopRDD[0] at textFile at <console>:21 []

scala> val mappedRdd = rdd.map(line => line++"")
mappedRdd: org.apache.spark.rdd.RDD[String] = MapPartitionsRDD[2] at ⏎
map at <console>:23

scala> mappedRdd.toDebugString
res1: String =
(2) MapPartitionsRDD[2] at map at <console>:23 []
 |   MapPartitionsRDD[1] at textFile at <console>:21 []
 |   spark-join.spark HadoopRDD[0] at textFile at <console>:21 []
```

We can see from above that, when discussing lineage, the way to actually display it is through the .toDebugString method.

Some examples of API commands that realize these RDDs are as follows:

```
scala> val rdd = sc.textFile("sample.txt")
rdd: org.apache.spark.rdd.RDD[String] = MapPartitionsRDD[1] at textFile ⏎
at <console>:21

scala> rdd.count
res0: Long = 7

scala> rdd.collect
res1: Array[String] = Array(1 2 3 4, 2 3 4 5, 3 4 5 6, 4 5 6 7, 5 6 7 8, ⏎
 6 7 8 9, 7 8 9 0)

scala> rdd.saveAsTextFile("out.txt")
```

Lineage is the exact capability for an RDD to continuously respond to failures within the system. When individual tasks fail and are relaunched by the resource scheduler of choice, those tasks look back within the lineage and determine what needs to be redone for the task to be considered complete.

Additional to their ability to track lineage, RDDs can *checkpoint* that lineage to disk. This acts as a metaphorical "save point" for the data, making it much easier to recompute failures at the task level, which is especially vital for long running Spark applications or applications working iteratively through large amounts of data. To gain the benefits of checkpointing refer to this code sample:

```scala
scala> sc.setCheckpointDir("checkpoint/")

scala> val rdd = sc.textFile("sample.txt")
rdd: org.apache.spark.rdd.RDD[String] = MapPartitionsRDD[20] at ↵
textFile at <console>:21

scala> val mappedRdd = rdd.map(line => line.split(" "))
mappedRdd: org.apache.spark.rdd.RDD[Array[String]] = MapPartitionsRDD ↵
[21] at map at <console>:23

scala> mappedRdd.collect
res14: Array[Array[String]] = Array(Array(1, 2, 3, 4),
Array(2, 3, 4, 5) ↵
, Array(3, 4, 5, 6), Array(4, 5, 6, 7), Array(5, 6, 7, 8),
Array(6, 7, 8, 9), Array(7, 8, 9, 0))

scala> val stringRdd = mappedRdd.map(a => a.toSet)
stringRdd: org.apache.spark.rdd.RDD[scala.collection.immutable.Set ↵
[String]] = MapPartitionsRDD[22] at map at <console>:25

scala> stringRdd.toDebugString
res15: String =
(2) MapPartitionsRDD[22] at map at <console>:25 []
 |  MapPartitionsRDD[21] at map at <console>:23 []
 |  MapPartitionsRDD[20] at textFile at <console>:21 []
 |  sample.txt HadoopRDD[19] at textFile at <console>:21 []

scala> stringRdd.checkpoint

scala> exit
warning: there were 1 deprecation warning(s); re-run with -deprecation ↵
for details

$ ls checkpoint/
29f75822-99dd-47ba-b9a4-5a36165e8885
```

In the above example we read in a small file, performed some computations on it, and then checkpointed the RDD, therefore maintaining the lineage on disk. The key to note is the bolded methods and primarily that of `sc.setCheckpointDir` that *must be set* before a checkpoint can occur. In the above example this directory was sitting locally, but if leveraging HDFS, this must be an HDFS path that the Spark application can reach.

It's also worthy to note that, if using the checkpointing feature within Spark, an RDD will need to be *computed twice* to perform the checkpoint. Therefore it's highly encouraged that developers execute .cache before the .checkpoint command.

One final piece of resiliency baked into the RDD paradigm is that it can seamlessly fall back to leveraging the disk for partitions that are too large to fit into memory. You can easily set this on their RDD with code such as:

```scala
scala> import org.apache.spark.storage.StorageLevel
import org.apache.spark.storage.StorageLevel

scala> val rdd = sc.textFile("sample.txt")
rdd: org.apache.spark.rdd.RDD[String] = MapPartitionsRDD[24] at ↵
textFile at <console>:24

scala> rdd.collect
res13: Array[String] = Array(1 2 3 4, 2 3 4 5, 3 4 5 6, 4 5 6 7, ↵
5 6 7 8, 6 7 8 9, 7 8 9 0)

scala> rdd.persist(StorageLevel.MEMORY_AND_DISK_SER)
res14: rdd.type = MapPartitionsRDD[24] at textFile at <console>:24
```

Refer to Table 5-1 to understand the various persistence modes that an RDD can leverage.

Table 5-1: RDD Persistence Modes

MEMORY_ONLY	Store the RDD as deserialized java objects, which are housed inside the JVM. If the entire RDD does not fit into memory, then some partitions will not be cached and recomputed on the fly. This is the default storage level for an RDD.
MEMORY_AND_DISK	Store the RDD as deserialized Java objects. For any partitions that do not fit in memory store them on disk and read them in when required.
MEMORY_ONLY_SER	Store the RDD as serialized Java objects with a single byte array per partition. This is typically more space efficient, although it comes at the CPU cost of serialization and deserialization when reading.
MEMORY_AND_DISK_SER	Similar to MEMORY_ONLY_SER, but for any partitions that do not fit in memory spill them to disk.
DISK_ONLY	Store the RDD as deserialized Java objects on disk only.
*_2 **(e.g., MEMORY_AND_DISK_2)**	By adding the _2 to any of the above levels you can duplicate each partition, with the storage level defined by which one chosen, onto two separate cluster nodes.
OFF_HEAP	Store the RDD in serialized format for the Apache Tachyon memory manager. This is attractive because it allows for many performance benefits such as reduced garbage collection.

The big question with persistence is always "which persistence level is best?" Normally the answer would be whatever works best for your application workload, but since we're focusing on a production application it is highly advised to forgo all other options and set the level to MEMORY_AND_DISK_SER. This is recommended for two reasons:

1. In a production environment it is assumed that the application is running on sufficiently scaled up hardware. Concretely, it is assumed that each machine in the cluster is, at minimum, housing 128GB of RAM, 16 physical CPU cores running at 2.5GHz, and 2TB of hard drive capacity spinning at 15,000 RPM. With that implementation you can safely assume that the impact of deserializing the Java objects back into memory from disk is negligible.

2. In production, things break. It's not a rarity, but a rule; and it's not that there isn't a developer out there who couldn't write a perfect application, but it's highly improbable. Knowing that, serializing state to disk is mandatory. When things fail it is imperative to have that state captured somewhere for retrieval. This is even more important when dealing with long running jobs. It also comes in when dealing with capacity planning. For instance, if the typical data load is 40GB a day (in memory) and it spikes to 300GB for some reason another day (for instance a denial of service attack), then having a disk-backed RDD can handle those anomalies with grace rather than with the Out Of Memory (OOM) exception.

There is one caveat to what was stated above and that involves latency requirements. When you have to go back to disk *and* deserialize the RDD to recover, it could be outside the latency window for some applications. In those low latency cases, typically involving Spark Streaming components, it can be much more beneficial to run the MEMORY_ONLY_2 option. This will reduce the risk of having an unrecoverable state by keeping everything in memory twice, but that poses a large risk if there is an overflow in data size. This mandates proper capacity planning for the system as it is being developed.

You could choose to leverage the MEMORY_AND_DISK_2 option, although that is a risk decision in the sense that, while the application might not fail, it might not meet its latency requirements. Again, this is purely a business decision, and, if unsure, both cases should be tested in parallel.

RDD Persistence Reassignment

When speaking of RDD persistence and the recommended storage it is helpful to note that odd errors can arise when attempting this for the first time—here we are discussing the issue of persistence reassignment. This can be a common issue when first dealing with RDD persistence and is one of the most common issues to fix. This is caused by an RDD having already been set with a given persistence level and then attempted to be reassigned. The following code snippet will demonstrate:

```
scala> import org.apache.spark.storage.StorageLevel
import org.apache.spark.storage.StorageLevel

scala> val rdd = sc.parallelize(Seq(Seq(1,2,3),Seq(2,3,4),Seq(3,4,5), ↵
Seq(4,5,6)))
rdd: org.apache.spark.rdd.RDD[Seq[Int]] = ParallelCollectionRDD[31] ↵
at parallelize at <console>:28

scala> rdd.persist(StorageLevel.MEMORY_AND_DISK_SER)
res15: rdd.type = ParallelCollectionRDD[31] at parallelize at ↵
<console>:28

scala> rdd.persist(StorageLevel.MEMORY_ONLY)
java.lang.UnsupportedOperationException: Cannot change storage
level of ↵
an RDD after it was already assigned a level
```

The resolution to this might not be as simple as it could be with larger projects, but the *only* resolution is to stop reassigning the persistence level *or* create a new RDD object that you can assign a new persistence level to. An example is as follows:

```
scala> import org.apache.spark.storage.StorageLevel
import org.apache.spark.storage.StorageLevel

scala> val rdd = sc.parallelize(Seq(Seq(1,2,3),Seq(2,3,4) ↵
,Seq(3,4,5),Seq(4,5,6)))
rdd: org.apache.spark.rdd.RDD[Seq[Int]] = ParallelCollectionRDD ↵
[0] at parallelize at <console>:22

scala> rdd.persist(StorageLevel.MEMORY_AND_DISK_SER)
res0: rdd.type = ParallelCollectionRDD[0] at parallelize at <console>:22

scala> val mappedRdd = rdd.map(line => line.toSet)
mappedRdd: org.apache.spark.rdd.RDD[scala.collection.immutable.Set ↵
[Int]] = MapPartitionsRDD[1] at map at <console>:24

scala> mappedRdd.persist(StorageLevel.MEMORY_ONLY)
res1: mappedRdd.type = MapPartitionsRDD[1] at map at <console>:24
```

A final note on persistence is that even though there are recommendations above, these are far from "silver bullets" to the general question of which is correct. In reality, only the developer of the application will understand the workload and boundary conditions, especially when migrating into production workloads. For instance, machine learning was not covered in either of the above, and, in those cases, repetition and possibly speed are key. For those workloads it would make sense to have an RDD persist only to memory for a series of time sensitive portions of the pipeline.

Now that we've covered the resilience of an RDD, it makes sense to briefly talk about the ability to implement your own version of an RDD (or modify the existing version). The RDD is, at its most basic level, merely an interface with five methods. You can refer to Table 5-2 on the five methods.

Table 5-2: RDD Methods

OPERATION	MEANING
`compute(Partition, TaskContext): Iterator`	Compute the elements of the given partition with respect to the task context provided.
`getPartitions(): Array[Partition]`	Retrieve a list of partitions for the given RDD. This method will only be called once; therefore, time-consuming operations can be implemented here.
`getDependencies(): Seq[Dependency[_]]`	Returns a list of dependencies that this RDD relies on. This method, like the one above, will only be called once; therefore, it is also safe for time-consuming operations.
`getPreferredLocations (Partition): Seq[String]`	Given a partition for an RDD, this will return a list of preferred locations for that partition.
`Partitioner: Option[Partitioner]`	A value that determines how this RDD is partitioned—typically either with a hash or range partitioning scheme.

Because an RDD relies on its ability to be partitioned, four of the five methods lie in the partition family. The last brings in the lineage topic and discusses the upstream dependencies (or parent RDDs) with which this RDD came from. This is necessary because the RDD is, and always will be, a *read-only* collection of records.

So, when developing a new RDD (such as what was done for the SchemaRDD) you will need to implement the above interface. This is paramount when discussing a production application with a proprietary data format thus leveraging an internal RDD implementation. You need to take care to understand your datasets when implementing the partitioning and ensure hotspots don't arise with default partition algorithms.

Batch versus Streaming

One large caveat that needs to be discussed is the difference between batch and streaming when it comes to fault tolerance. While Spark Streaming is just one component of the Spark ecosystem, it lives in a slightly different world when compared against the rest of the Spark components.

When dealing with streaming applications their fault tolerance and behavior is magnified because of the constant change of state. Depending on the usage of the streaming system further changes its qualities. For instance, an ingestion application that reads in millions of ad clicks and stores them into a database for analytic usage is much different than a system that takes in a users' page views and returns a score with how likely that page is to contain malicious content.

So how does a streaming solution differ? First, within Spark, data is now represented as a microbatch of data (called DStreams) and operations on those RDDs are only that individual microbatch (except window operations). When thinking with a microbatch mindset you now need to worry about the following key aspects of your application:

- **Understand the throughput of the system**—Specifically understand the rate and size of the messages entering the system. This is part of a larger capacity planning effort that needs to live with the streaming system, but more concretely, this will determine the load on the system at any given moment and its external frameworks (if any).

- **When testing, run the system for twice as long as your oldest piece of data plus one**—Most streaming solutions want to house everything, and, in that case, we've seen a minimum of two weeks running straight through to suffice for most issues. In the case where data is actually aged off, make sure to run the system for, at minimum, twice that length. For instance, if the system houses application data for 30 days, run the system for 61 days. This ensures that two roll off periods hit and they are successful.

- **Understand the latency window for each microbatch**—Spark can get down to 500 milliseconds per window, but it's key to understand what the worst-case time is that can still be acceptable and to test those cases, especially in failure scenarios (see the Availability Tests section for more details).

The largest difference between batch and streaming applications is the concept of *how* the data enters the system. With traditional Spark applications the RDD maintains the fault tolerant properties we discussed above, those being immutability and deterministic recomputability through data lineage. But, those properties change when discussing Spark Streaming applications.

Within streaming applications, data is received through the concept of Receivers. These are components that receive data over the network (except for the fileStream Receiver) and thus change their reliability properties. To achieve similar results with typical RDDs streaming Receivers replicate the data received across the cluster (twice by default) into different worker nodes.

This creates two new scenarios that need to be considered.

1. Data survives the copy onto one worker node, but fails to get copied into another. This arises when one of the worker nodes fails for some reason before the copy of data could be completed.

2. Data is received and buffered by a single input source, but fails before it can copy the data to another Receiver. In this case the failure requires that a Receiver be able to recover the lost data back from the originating source. This is the trickier of the two solutions.

Building on the above two scenarios, Spark maintains the concept of *reliable* and *unreliable* Receivers. The Spark documentation describes the two beautifully and is repeated below:

Reliable Receiver—**These receivers acknowledge reliable sources only after ensuring that the received data has been replicated. If such a receiver fails, the source will not receive acknowledgment for the buffered (unreplicated) data. Therefore, if the receiver is restarted, the source will resend the data, and no data will be lost due to the failure.**

Unreliable Receiver—**Such receivers do *not* send acknowledgment and therefore *can* lose data when they fail due to worker or driver failures.**

Further, when considering data loss with the various Receiver types, you need to understand what happens in the event of a worker or driver failure. Table 5-3 describes each based on the Receiver type.

Table 5-3: Receiver Types

	WORKER FAILURE	DRIVER FAILURE
Reliable Receiver	No data loss. Data can be replayed from the originating input source.	All past data that was received and replicated *in memory* will be lost.
Unreliable Receiver	Any data received (buffered) that was not replicated is lost.	All past data that was received and replicated *in memory* will be lost including any current data recently buffered.

Another key feature of Spark Streaming that was introduced with Spark 1.2 is the concept of a write-ahead log. These are stateful log files that are persisted to disk of each action or event that the system is *going to perform*.

An example of this would be when a reliable Receiver is about to grab a message off an upstream queue. It would write in the write-ahead log that it is about to pull in message X with some ID Y. Then, if the system were to fail before the operation could be completed, it would be able to check the write-ahead log once it was brought back online to determine where it left off.

When write-ahead logging is enabled (by default it is not) then there is zero data loss under both driver and worker failures. This, however, leads to *at-least-once* processing semantics, which can be confusing when migrating a Spark Streaming application from development to production.

Diving into processing semantics quickly, there are three main types, and Spark Streaming supports two of the three depending on the type of Receiver implemented. They are as follows:

1. *At-least-once* **processing**—This is where each message or record entering the system is processed *at least once* by the system. It is up to the application developer to ensure that, if the message is seen *more than once*, the application understands how to handle those scenarios.

2. *At-most-once* **semantics**—For each message entering the system it will be processed *at most once*. This scenario is not supported in the Spark Streaming paradigm.

3. *Exactly-once* **processing guarantees**—It means that for each message entering the system it will only be processed *exactly once* even in the event of a failure. This is hardest to support, but it is typically what is seen when initially developing Spark Streaming applications because of the input Receiver being a sort of test file on a file system.

To enable write-ahead logs see the following code example:

```
import org.apache.spark._
import org.apache.spark.streaming._

val conf = SparkConf()
    .setMaster("local[4]")
    .setAppName("<your-app-name-here>")
    .set("spark.streaming.receiver.writeAheadLog.enable", "true")
    .set("spark.streaming.receiver.writeAheadLog
    .rollingIntervalSecs",    "1")
val sc = new SparkContext(conf)
val ssc = new StreamingContext(sc, Seconds(1))
```

Note that the above example should be leveraged within application code and *not* run within the Spark shell like other examples. This is because, in this example, we are explicitly creating a new SparkContext; and StreamingContext; so, if ran inside of the Spark shell, it would produce an error and fail because a SparkContext already exists inside that JVM.

Testing Strategies

This is where the rubber meets the road. Not many people like to test at this scale, but it is absolutely necessary when taking an application into production. We'll cover various methodologies, but, as we've seen before, it is up to the business and developers to determine which of the many strategies are best for the given application. Typically these are based around funding decisions, as some of the concepts can be quite expensive to roll out and/or maintain over time.

One facet to this is the advent of Amazon Web Services (AWS) and other cloud offerings as a means to spin up arbitrarily large clusters to test and deploy your application without the need of owning the hardware internally. This can be a great asset, but as with all things, nothing is free. Once testing scales into the hundreds of machines with large amounts of RAM, it is necessary to measure the cost of running the machines against the necessity of the test being performed.

Within testing, one necessary component that every developer dreads is the test plan. While never exciting, it helps to scope the work that needs to be completed and acts as a reference guide to the various scaling milestones. Once an application is denoted as ready to move into the production lifecycle, this should be one of the first documents created so that the application can begin its testing phases as soon as possible.

Unit Tests

These are the tests that everyone has heard of. They are set up to ensure code and individual functions are covered and operate adequately within expected limitations (negative numbers, zeros, empty strings, etc.). Since there is so much documentation out there for these types of tests we won't spend much time covering them.

Integration Tests

Integration tests are the first line of defense in nontraditional testing. We say nontraditional in that nearly all developers understand the concept of unit testing to some extent or other, but integration tests are usually the first stage filter where developers drop off and lose familiarity.

Integrations tests are roughly defined as tests that incorporate external entities or platforms. It is highly unlikely that the application being developed is built in a box and doesn't use any other library or service to function, especially in today's highly connected world. This means, for each external service used, tests should be written to ensure connectivity, usage patterns, etc. are functioning properly.

To solidify this concept, think of a Spark Streaming application that leverages Apache Kafka for its upstream message queue. In this paradigm you would want to test that the Spark application can perform a set of functions with the Kafka message broker such as:

- Can the application connect successfully to the message broker as a single instance? Can it connect to a multinode message broker?

- Can the application read a message successfully from the queue? Does that message come in a format the system understands?

- Can the application survive when the message broker becomes unreachable?

- How does the application handle upstream broker errors?

The above is not an exhaustive list by any means, but hopefully it provides a context to what it means to provide integration tests.

If developing your Spark application in Scala there are a few great integration frameworks out there such as `scalatest`, the Play framework (found at `https://www.playframework.com/`), and `sbt`. For Java, the clear winner for most is the JUnit framework paired with the Mockito library. And finally, if developing in Python, there are the `unittest` and `pytest` frameworks available although there is much to be desired when looking in those departments.

Durability Tests

This is likely the first series of tests that aren't necessarily known or well documented. Durability tests mandate that the application accept some series of defined input and return an equivalent series of defined output. While this might seem simple and be covered through various unit tests, durability tests always dictate scale.

To properly ensure durability tests are performed properly, especially with a production application mindset, you need to scale the application across a large enough number of segregated machines to mimic a production environment. The term "segregated" here means that we need to leverage separate machines networked together. These could be virtual machines in the case of cloud providers or physical machines across a rack (or multiple racks), but must reside in different areas. This ensures that network pathways are leveraged properly just as in a production environment.

Often it's asked, "Can I just virtualize the application on my laptop?" and the resounding answer is no. Spark specifically optimizes differently, based on its layout across the cluster, and, while virtualization can help understand bottlenecks and issues, it is a Band-Aid to properly emulating a production environment. Networking errors can and will occur. It is paramount to ensure that the system can correctly handle these errors in at-scale environments.

To properly set up a durability test you need a few things.

- **An environment that can sufficiently emulate production**—Here we specifically mean cluster layout, but not necessarily size. If, for instance, the production environment is a 50-node cluster (where 50 is the number of data nodes), you could easily run a durability test at 50% of the at-scale production cluster. So, in this example, a cluster size of 25 data nodes would be sufficient to execute a proper test. As a general rule of thumb, durability tests run with, at minimum, 50% of the expected nodes that are needed in the end-state environment.

- **A sufficient and representative amount of data**—This data should be highly cataloged and understood. The key to a durability test is to quantitatively state that for every element fed into the system there is a correct and corresponding response. This is exacerbated when discussing streaming solutions.

Let's walk through an example to further solidify what we've stated above. Say the Spark application is leveraging the GraphX component where each node is an individual user and each edge is a connection between two users (a social network graph). See Figure 5-2 as an example.

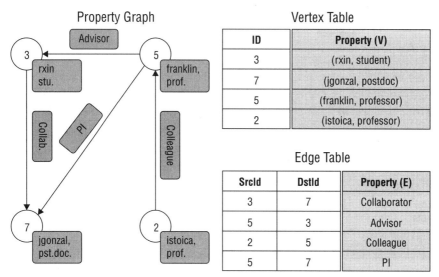

Figure 5-2: Simple property graph (from `http://spark.apache.org/docs/latest/graphx-programming-guide.html`)

This application accepts queries of users, and the response from the system is then all of the outward edges from the node supplied. With the above example in mind, if you were to query for rxin, the response would be the list of one element being [`jgonzal`]. Again, if you queried for franklin, the response would be [`rxin, jgonzal`].

To build a durability test from this type of application you would do the following:

1. **Write an application to generate data that will populate the system (a graph in this instance)**—Data generated for this example could be in the form of <user> <user> where each pair is the outward connection of the first user to the second user.

2. **Populate a new system with the aforementioned dataset**—This is done to ensure that the state of the system is completely known and there are no side-effects before the test starts.

3. **For each line in the generated dataset query the system for the expected response**—This is the critical piece. In this example, which because of the nature of a graph is on the tougher side to represent, there will be multiple responses of the same value, but the *check to ensure their validity will change.* This is because, with a graph system, the population of the system is typically in the form of N ⇨ M where M < N. This merely means that there is less information stored than what is originally provided. *This property will change based on the system.* Some systems may have *more* information based on the population of their state, while some may equal out (typical streaming solutions). So, for this example, you would iterate over each line in the generated dataset with the first <user> and, with the response, check the list for the existence of the second <user>.

One point of note about the first bullet is that, when generating the dataset, it should be representative of the dataset expected within production. While this can be a difficult thing to do there are a few pointers to this:

- **Data in production is not uniformly random**—That said; do not generate data with a random generator. If you have users, like the above example, then either find a library or build something that represents the population. Or, even better, pull down historical census data and use those names.

- **Always generate more data than you need**—If the system is expected to hold 2TB of data, be prepared to generate at least 50% more. This may not be explicitly necessary for a durability test, but it will be necessary for other tests, and, if the generation of data was difficult, it's best to get more than you need on the first go.

To restate, the entire goal of the durability test is to ensure that, for some known state of the system, all pathways are worked and all responses are correct for every input. If this is not accomplished, then the durability test is not complete. Moreover each system is different. Developing a core Spark application that runs a machine learning job through MLlib will be very different from a Spark Streaming job that calculates click-through, and that will be very different from a GraphX job as seen above.

Fuzzing Tests

Fuzzing tests have historically been a mainstream component of testing for Security professionals, and they very much earn a place in the development of scalable and large production applications. If you happen to be a security professional then feel free to skip right over this section.

Fuzzing, in general, is a methodology of testing whereby you do not give known good inputs to the system, but rather utter gibberish (somewhat). If the system takes as input a user as an ASCII-encoded string, what happens if you give it characters outside of its range of capability (like this series of symbols (چیاکـــاش))? If the system takes a single integer as input, what happens when you give it an integer out of its bounds (an integer overflow)?

Often these types of tests are forgotten, and, thus, security students flourish at hackathons where they can break your application for a bit of cash. That said, to make it *that much* harder for them, why not perform some of these a priori to launch?

One of the nice features of fuzzing tests, is that they work both as systemic checks against the system as a whole (viewed as a black box) as well as integrated into unit tests. These tests can be viewed as ways to measure and validate both *internal* and *external* fault tolerance.

When developing successful fuzzing tests, it is often better to develop a framework that supplies *random* input into the system, rather than explicitly calling various system functions with "inverse" inputs (numbers when functions accept strings and vice versa). Below are a few tips:

- **Develop a framework to test all public functions**—This, like unit testing, is meant to ensure proper code coverage.

- **The more randomness the better**—Do not put any limits on the randomness of the generated input that will be sent to the system. Specifically, we're saying randomness should come from both the type of input as well as the length.

The overall goal of fuzzing tests is to understand where the system breaks, how it handles random input, and where the system becomes nondeterministic. These tests typically make the system act in very odd ways and can even corrupt file systems and data if not careful. If at all possible, it is best to run these types of tests in isolated environments and segregated from any critical resources (hardware, networking, data, etc.).

Availability Tests

Availability tests are likely the hardest tests to write because they take so much time to do correctly. So much so that Netflix open sourced its own library called Chaos Monkey (information found at `https://github.com/Netflix/SimianArmy/wiki/Chaos-Monkey`) to do just this style of testing.

What is an availability test? It is one in which the system is tested against loss of key services to ensure that it can still provide a correct response in a healthy amount of time. In simpler terms, it can be thought of as testing failover, and, with Spark, this involves loss of the Spark master, driver, and workers, but it is not inclusive of only those elements. For any external frameworks that your application leverages, so too do those pieces need to be tested.

For instance, if the system checkpoints periodically to HDFS, then you should ensure that, with a comparable availability test, the Name Node gets taken down (Nodes if in high availability mode) as well as various Data Nodes.

The best part about an availability test is that to get started with simple tests is quite easy (assuming you've completed the durability portion). This is because you can run the durability test and, while running, start rebooting machines with key assets. Now, this certainly isn't the recommended way to perform these tests, but acts as a "fast and dirty" first approach. For any application looking to move into production this set of tests should be paramount.

Another facet that needs to be measured with the availability tests should be the response time of the system. When most systems go to production, they have that pesky service level agreement attached to them, and, within that, there is a minimum response time for the system else it falls outside its SLA window. The availability test *absolutely should measure the response times under all failure scenarios*.

Now, to develop an at-scale series of availability tests, you should read the following bits of advice:

- **Automate everything**—This is DevOps 101, but is even more so here. Being able to automate the kill -9 of a given service is great, but what's even better is being able to bring it up and down cleanly, uncleanly, and during random moments of load.

- **More randomness is better**—Unlike the data generation tip, more randomness tends to be better here as the developer will typically only instrument the test so far and tends to skew towards bringing specific applications down at what they would consider "critical moments." This only allows the system to be tested under specific conditions and, very likely, will not find all issues.

- **Ensure that multiple services go down at once**—Having a system that can handle any individual service being down is great, but truly understanding *where a system breaks* is what this test should actually demonstrate. If developers are afraid to have multiple services crash at once then it's more likely that it needs to happen.

To conclude, the goal of an availability test is solely to test the system against service failures of all types. This style of testing is paramount when migrating an application into production.

Recommended Configurations

This is the final section within fault tolerance, and, with that, we're going to cover the last piece on how to tune your Spark application such that it can not only survive, but also thrive in a production landscape.

At this point all of these configurations are going to be highly independent of what is necessary *for your application* and what isn't. These are not silver bullets, but merely common recommendations from what has been seen "in the field." It is highly encouraged that, for each configuration change, you run the gamut of test suites covered above to check and measure whether there is a notable increase in fault tolerance or degradation in performance.

Further, we are not going to look at common configurations for each of the major Spark components. It is highly unlikely that, when delving into Spark, you are *only* using the core API, although, when configuring Spark, nearly all configurations apply across the board to the component projects as well. For the few that don't, we leave that as an exercise to the reader to determine. As a note, since Bagel is a deprecated package and, at the time of this writing, is being discussed on whether it will exist in Spark 2.0, we do not provide any configuration assistance. It is recommended that all Bagel applications look to migrate to the more stable and actively supported GraphX module.

Spark Core

With Spark Core there are a number of parameters that should be taken into consideration when looking at migrating an application into production. This will cover a majority of the issues when looking at other areas and components of Spark as well. We, however, will not cover any configurations related to security in this section because those issues are covered in the next chapter. We will, however, focus on all configurations that aid in increasing the *fault tolerance* and *reliability* of the application (see Table 5-4).

Table 5-4: A List of Configuration Parameters for Spark Configuration

APPLICATION PROPERTIES	DESCRIPTION
`spark.driver.cores`	The number of cores to use for the driver application when in "cluster" mode for resource management. The default is one and, in production hardware, can very likely be scaled up to 8 or 16 at minimum.
`spark.driver.maxResultSize`	If the application is leveraging the driver heavily, it is advised to set this number higher than its default of "1g." A value of 0 will mean unlimited. This value reflects the max size of all partitions for any Spark action.
`spark.driver.memory`	Total amount of memory for the driver process. As with the number of cores it's advisable to set this number to "16g" or "32g" based on your application and hardware. The default is "1g."
`spark.executor.memory`	The amount of memory to use per executor process, which also defaults to "1g." This should be brought up to "4g," "8g," "16g," or higher based on the hardware of the cluster.

APPLICATION PROPERTIES	DESCRIPTION
`spark.local.dir`	Where Spark natively writes its local files including RDD's stored on disk. This should be a fast access disk although it defaults to "/tmp." It is highly recommended to set this to somewhere with fast storage disks (SSD's preferred) and moderate to large amounts of space. In the event of serializing objects to disk it will fall to this location, and, if there is no space, it is nondeterministic what would happen with the application.

Runtime Environment

`spark.executor.logs .rolling.*`	There are four properties that set up and maintain rolling logs within Spark. These properties should be set if the Spark application is meant to run for long periods of time—the general consensus is greater than 24 hours.
`spark.python.worker .memory`	If using Python for the Spark application this property will allocate the total amount of memory for each Python worker process. It defaults to "512m."

Shuffle Behavior

`spark.shuffle .manager`	This is the implementation method for shuffling data within Spark that defaults to "sort." The only reason it's referenced here is to note that, if the application is leveraging Apache Tungsten, then you should set this to "tungsten-sort."
`spark.shuffle .memoryFraction`	This is the fraction of Java heap space to leverage for shuffle operations before spilling to disk with a default of "0.2." If the application is spilling frequently or if multiple shuffle operations are happening it is recommended to raise this higher. Typically you go from "0.2" to "0.4" and then "0.6" to ensure everything stabilizes. It is not recommended to go beyond "0.6" as it can get in the way and contend with other objects on the heap.
`spark.shuffle .service.enabled`	Enables the external shuffle service within Spark. This is necessary if utilizing dynamic allocation for scheduling. It is set to "false" by default.

Compression and Serialization

`spark.kryo .classesToRegister`	When utilizing Kryo for object serialization you need to register those classes. Set this property for all custom objects the application uses that Kryo will serialize.
`spark.kryo .registrator`	Use this instead of the above if the custom classes needing serialization extend the "KryoRegistrator" class.
`spark.rdd.compress`	Sets whether the serialized RDDs should be compressed or not. By default, this is set to false, but as stated above, with adequate hardware this should be enabled, as the CPU performance hit should be negligible.

Continues

Table 3-4 (*continued*)

APPLICATION PROPERTIES	DESCRIPTION
`spark.serializer`	Set this to use the Kryo serialization method rather than the default, which are the Java-based versions. It is *highly* recommended to configure Kryo for serialization over the default as this is one of the best performance and stability improvements you can make.
Execution Behavior	
`spark.cleaner.ttl`	Duration in seconds of how long Spark will remember any metadata for its objects. By default, this is set to "infinite" and, for long running jobs, can act as a memory leak. Tune accordingly. It is best to set this at "3600" and monitor performance from there.
`spark.executor.cores`	The number of cores to set for each executor. This value defaults based on the resource scheduler chosen. If using YARN or standalone cluster mode this value should be tuned.
Networking	
`spark.akka.frameSize`	The maximum message size in Spark cluster communication. When running across a large dataset with thousands of map and reduce tasks, this number should be raised from "128" to "512" or higher.
`spark.akka.threads`	The number of Akka threads to use for communication. With a driver application running multiple cores it is recommended to increase this from "4" to "16," "32" or higher.
Scheduling	
`spark.cores.max`	Sets the maximum number of CPU cores to request for the application from all nodes across the cluster. If running on a resource-constrained environment, then this should be set to, at most, the number of cores available to Spark on the cluster.

Again, this list is not exhaustive of the total number of configuration parameters you can configure with Spark, but it provides an overview of what we've seen as the most important ones to start investigating on the journey to production. To view the complete list of configuration parameters, see the Spark documentation page at `http://spark.apache.org/docs/latest/configuration.html`.

Summary

We've covered a lot in this chapter, from major architectural components of Spark that make up its ability to be fault tolerant to the various configuration options for Spark Core. But this is a journey that is just beginning. If you're reading this book and already have an application in mind that you want to take to production or are currently working on one, then take a step back and look at your application thus far and how it sizes up to what we've discussed. Some questions that should have answers:

- What is the service level agreement of my application?
- What are the risks to the business if my application *does not* meet its service level agreement?
- What are all of the components being used within the application? Are *all* of them required?
- What are the *internal* and *external* fault tolerance guarantees that my application must support?
- What are the edge cases of the application thus far? If *none*, has the application been adequately tested?

The above are just a few of many questions that should be assessed. It is imperative that you learn, understand, and possibly define, if necessary, your individual checklist for your company *and application*. Each application has a separate journey on its path to production and more so its own journey of becoming fault tolerant to all *threats*.

At the end of the day fault tolerance is in direct correlation with that of the security of the application, as you'll see in Chapter 6. This is because, and we haven't used the term until now, your application does not know the difference between an interaction (remember external fault tolerance?) and a threat. Therefore you need to assess all interactions as threat vectors that *can affect the fault tolerance of the system.*

Beyond Spark

There are several techniques required to run Spark effectively that have been covered in previous chapters. They are the preparation for running Spark jobs. So it is now time to run our Spark application. Usually, this is a machine learning algorithm or an aggregation of some log data, or a business intelligence workload. Spark can be applied in many areas, including Business Intelligence, data warehousing, recommendation, fraud detection, and more. Spark has a large and growing community, as well as ecosystems that are indispensable in enterprise environments. These ecosystems provide many functionalities that are evident in various production use cases. Of course we first need to understand how to use Spark with the external libraries that are active contributors in the first place!

In this chapter, we'll introduce you to the Spark case studies and frameworks covering topics such as data warehousing and machine learning. These are areas where Spark can really help you solve problems. Although Spark is a relatively new tool, there are various kinds of use cases that exist, which we will cover. These frameworks are crucial for your Spark applications, so follow along as we explore them.

Data Warehousing

Data analysis is the core process required for making progress of any kind in business. The data warehousing system is a significant system for this type of analysis. Thanks to a lot of frameworks and ecosystems, Spark can be a core component to provide data warehousing functionality in your enterprise environment. This is shown in Figure 6-1. Of course Spark provides this functionality at a large scale differently than other existing tools. SQL is the fine-grained data analysis method used by a lot of data analysts, data scientists, and engineers. Spark can be used as a data warehouse framework supporting SQL processing, called Spark SQL.

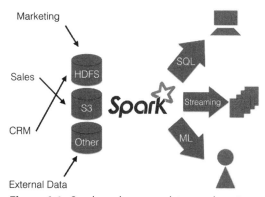

Figure 6-1: Spark can be a core data warehousing component.

Spark core is already integrated into other distributed filesystems such as HDFS, S3. If you have business data in such a system already, it is easy to transfer the existing business processes into Spark, because all you need to do is launch the Spark cluster with your data storage system. Spark also provides a developer-friendly API that you can access with Python and R that are supported by data scientists, and have been for quite some time. If you are used to these languages already, it isn't difficult to select Spark as your own Data Warehousing engine.

You will be able to process larger datasets on Spark without losing your familiar interface. The unique interface of Spark SQL is DataFrame, which is inspired by the R language. It is recommended that you use this interface when accessing structured data with Spark. DataFrame will be covered in detail in the next section. Let's examine a pure SQL interface. Spark provides roughly three types of data warehousing functionalities: SparkSQL, DataFrame, and Hive on Spark. As mentioned previously, DataFrame is related to the machine learning pipeline, though it is originally developed with Spark SQL. It will be introduced together with ML/MLlib. In this section we will cover Spark SQL and Hive on Spark, focusing on how to set up the cluster. Before trying these

SQL functionalities in Spark, you must download the pre-build package with the Hive profile, or build the package using the Hive profile. If you choose to build the Spark package by yourself, the build command is as follows:

```
$ build/mvn -Pyarn -Phive -Phive-thriftserver \
            -Phadoop-2.6.0 -Dhadoop.version=2.6.0 \
            -DskipTests clean package
```

Please make sure to install Zinc, which is a long running server that aims to be an increment compiler for sbt. If you are using OS X, you can install with brew install zinc.

After running this build command, you can obtain a Spark package build with Hive classes. As you can see, the Hadoop version can be easily selected with a -P profile and -Dhadoop.version. It is better to select the version according to your target Hadoop cluster or Hive functionalities. In other words, if you are trying to use Hive 0.13 running on Hadoop 2.7.0, your build command looks like the following:

```
$ build/mvn -Pyarn -Phive -Phive-thriftserver \
            -Phadoop-2.7.0 -Dhadoop.version=2.7.0 \
            -DskipTests clean package
```

Spark SQL CLI

Using the Spark SQL CLI is the easiest way to try Spark SQL on your local machine. This convenient tool launches the Hive metastore in local mode and receives your SQL queries. Hive metastore is a storage system prepared for meta information of each database and tables. In production usage, the metastore must be hosted by an RDBMS system such as MySQL. In this case we can omit it because spark-sql launches local metastore automatically. Like the hive command, it may be good to use it to investigate functionality, but not in production. All you have to do is type the following command under the Spark directory.

```
$ ./bin/spark-sql
  ...
    spark-sql>
```

There might be several type logs in the console. After the flood of debug and info logs, you can check to see if the prompt of Spark SQL CLI shows up.

Thrift JDBC/ODBC Server

Spark implements thrift servers such as HiveServer2. HiveServer2 is an interface daemon waiting to submit your query. You can access the HiveServer2 through the JDBC/ODBC interface. This means that you can access the Spark SQL engine through your existing JDBC/ODBC server or BI tools, which provides some cost savings. You don't need to prepare new connecting tools for your analytics team of sales team. In order to launch the Thrift server, please type this command, which is included in the Spark directory:

```
$ ./sbin/start-thriftserver.sh
```

This command launches the Thrift server to run a SQL driver. By default, the server is launched at `localhost:10000`. You can change this port number and other configurations. To test the Thrift server, you should use the `beeline` included in the Spark directory, which is a simple command-line tool for submitting Hive queries, although `beeline` was not originally developed by the Hive project:

```
$ ./bin/beeline
```

`beeline` is a JDBC client. By using this, you can automatically access the Thrift server with only specifying the hostname and port number. Type the following command if you didn't change the default port number for the Thrift server:

```
beeline> !connect jdbc:hive2://localhost:10000
```

At this stage, `beeline` asks you to enter your username and password. If you run Thrift server in nonsecure mode, only the username is required.

Hive on Spark

Apache Hive is data warehousing software for managing large datasets in distributed storage such as HDFS. Hive was originally developed as a simple interface for manipulating Hadoop MapReduce tasks. Hive has also a long history, almost as much as Hadoop's history. After that, Tez was introduced as a more flexible and reliable framework, which tried to replace the MapReduce framework. Apache Tez is a general distributed execution engine that is more sophisticated than MapReduce. Since Tez aims to be a general execution engine, we can use it as a SQL execution engine if the execution plan is correctly created. Hive already supported this framework as well, in addition to MapReduce. Since Hive 1.1, Hive also supports Spark as a query execution engine. That means Hive currently supports three execution engines: Hadoop MapReduce, Tez, and Spark. Although it is not fully completed and it's still under active development (details and progresses are in HIVE-7292), Hive can now make use of the speed and reliability of Spark. Here is a process to try Hive on Spark on your local machine.

At the beginning, it is necessary to start the Spark cluster. Note that you must download a version of Spark that does not include Hive JARs. In order to exclude Hive JARs from the Spark package by yourself, you type the following:

```
$ ./make-distribution.sh --name hadoop2-without-hive \
                    --tgz -Pyarn -Phadoop-2.6 \
                    -Pparquet-provided
```

With this command you can build your own Spark package without Hive JARs. But the easiest way to launch a Spark cluster on YARN is to use the ec2 script included in the Spark directory:

```
$ ./ec2/spark-ec2 —key-pair=<Your key pair name> \
                    —identity-file=<Your key pair path> \
                    --region=us-east-1 --zone=us-east-1a\
                    —hadoop-major-version=yarn \
                    launch hive-on-spark-cluster
```

The details of how to use the spark-c2 script is written in the Spark official document (https://spark.apache.org/docs/latest/ec2-scripts.html). The script is written for making it easy to launch Spark clusters on EC2 instances. It requires taking AWS accounts and getting AWS key pairs issued from an AWS console. The details can be read from the above document.

After a few minutes, you will have a Spark cluster running on YARN. The cluster does not include Hive as a default. You need to install the Hive package onto the Spark cluster. Hive can be downloaded into this Spark master server, and then you launch it with Hive CLI:

```
wget http://ftp.yz.yamagata-u.ac.jp/pub/network/apache/hive/hive-1.1.1/ ⏎
apache-hive-1.1.1-bin.tar.gz
$ tar zxvf apache-hive-1.1.1-bin.tar.gz
$ cd apache-hive-1.1.1-bin.tar.gz
$ bin/hive
hive> set spark.home=/location/to/sparkHome;
hive> set hive.execution.engine=spark;
```

The process described above might be troublesome when you want to try Hive on Spark, because there are some cases where a conflict occurs between the Hadoop and Hive version when you launch the Hadoop cluster by yourself. So, you should consider using some distribution such as CDH or HDP, which includes both Hive and Spark and the compatibility and functionality between each component has been tested. This is the shortest route, but it is important to know which component is dependent on the other components, given that this is under active development and the components have complicated dependencies on each other.

Machine Learning

Machine learning plays a pivotal role in the next generation data processing area in the Big Data technology field. Collecting a lot of data can have a significant effect on performance. This means that collecting a lot of data using the power of processing can make a good machine learning model. Hadoop and its ecosystems are realizing the basic environment (machine learning with big data) by providing a simple and generic distributed framework. Spark enhanced this trend even more. So we want to focus on the usage of machine learning algorithms and concrete job creating processes in this chapter. Of course Spark wasn't developed only for machine learning. But its on-memory processing architecture is a great fit for tackling machine learning problems. In this section, as our next use case, we will focus on machine learning in Spark. Machine learning itself is not easy for developers at first glance due to the mathematics and complex theories. There is some knowledge and some preconditions that are required to use the machine learning algorithm efficiently on Spark. Here are the main machine learning concepts that we will cover:

- The DataFrame framework, which makes it easy to create and manipulate realistic structured data. This framework provides a sophisticated interface, which enables you to forget the difference of each machine learning algorithm and optimization. Thanks to the fixed data schema, DataFrame can optimize its own workload to fit the data.

- MLlib and ML are core machine learning frameworks integrated into Spark. These frameworks are external in nature, but they are fully compatible and can be used seamlessly with the Spark core because they are maintained by the core Spark committer team.

- Other external machine learning frameworks that can be used on Spark include Mahout and Hivemall. Both of them support the current Spark engine. In the cases that MLlib and ML cannot cover, these external libraries can be an option.

DataFrame

DataFrame is originally the concept of the R language (called `data.frame` in R), and has been applied to Python frameworks such as Pandas. DataFrame is like a table that is organized into named columns. Real-world data is often stored into some kind of structured format in order to be processed by SQL processing. You can train machine learning models transparently with this data by using DataFrame. It is a good thing to extract data as a DataFrame, because Spark provides the general distributed processing framework. You don't need to care about the scalability of performance and rewrite the code to scale to fit in large scale datasets at the distributed environment even in the DataFrame context. You are able to use the same code at the development for testing or debugging and production stages for providing user services. DataFrame can be created from RDD, Hive tables, and JSON. Since DataFrame supports a lot of data formats already, your data may already be included. This means you are able to use DataFrame with your data immediately. The first thing you must do is create `SQLContext`. This class manages the usage of DataFrame. Of course it is okay to use any class that inherits `SQLContext`. This class can be created from `SparkContext` as you can see here:

```
// it is already defined if you use
// spark-shell tool.
val sc: SparkContext
// sqlContext is also defined in spark-shell
val sqlContext = new org.apache.spark.sql.SQLContext(sc)
// This is necessary to convert an RDD to a DataFrame
// implicitly
import sqlContext.implicits._
```

There is an additional feature in SparkSQL here. You can use HiveQL as well. HiveQL is a dialect of SQL developed for Hive and it has a lot of unique functionality and user defined functions. In order to use HiveQL, `HiveContext` also needs to be created like `SparkContext`, which is a superset of `SQLContext`. SparkSQL supports dialect features that can parse some variation of SQL using the `spark.sql.dialect` option. The only dialect available with this option is `sql` provided by Spark SQL currently. When you use `HiveContext`, the default parameter is `hiveql`.

There are some data files that can be used for DataFrame in the Spark directory, allowing you then to use this data as a DataFrame sample. This data is put under `examples/src/main/resources/`.

```
// DataFrame can read a json file without specifying the
// schema explicitly
val df = sqlContext.read ↵
    .json("examples/src/main/resources/people.json")
df.show()
// age  name
// null Michael
// 30   Andy
// 19   Justin
```

DataFrame features can be used as other API components through Scala, Java, Python, and R. Here is some code in Scala that is assumed to be the most popular language for the usage with Spark. DataFrame provides a SQL-like interface to users. For example, when you access all of the names of the above people data, you can do it like this:

```
df.select("name").show()
// name
// Michael
// Andy
// Justin
```

DataFrame can be converted into RDD, which is traditionally used in the Spark data distributed processing. There are two ways to convert RDD into DataFrame. The first one is inferring DataFrame schema using the JVM reflection system. DataFrame has a structure like a SQL table, but we do not need to specify the scheme thanks to this inferring system. Specifically in Scala, you can use the `case` class to infer the schema of a given RDD. The `case` class in Scala is a unique class that can generate a fixed structure and its own accessor to members automatically (see `http://docs.scala-lang.org/tutorials/tour/case-classes.html`). If you use Scala as a Spark interface, this might be the easiest way:

```
case class Person(name: String, age: Int)
val people = sc.textFile("examples/src/main/resources/people.txt")
  .map(_.split(",")).map(p => Person(p(0), p(1).trim.toInt)).toDF()
people.select("name").show()
```

The second way is converting RDD by specifying the data type. Each element inside `people.txt` can be converted with the `map` method with RDD easily, and this can play a role in defining the schema of this table by using the `case` class in Scala. Secondly, you can convert RDD into DataFrame by specifying the schema with `org.apache.spark.sql.type.*`:

```
val people = sc.textFile("examples/src/main/resources/⏎
        people.txt")
import org.apache.spark.sql.type.{StructType, StructField, StringType}
// Definition of data schema
val schema = StructType(Seq(
    StructField("name", StringType, true),
    StructField("age", StringType, true)))
// First import as Row class
val rowRDD = people.map(_.split(",")) ⏎
    .map(p => Row(p(0), p(1).trim))
// Create DataFrame with the previous definition
val peopleDataFrame = sqlContext ⏎
    .createDataFrame(rowRDD, schema)
```

Generally, it is easier to use the inferring method to convert RDD into DataFrame because of the amount of necessary code to be written. There are, however, some cases where you want more flexibility to define your own DataFrame.

For example, in Scala 2.10 it is not supported to define the `case` class with more than 22 member fields. This is the restriction by Scala itself. In this case, it is necessary to define your own custom table with `StructTypes` programmatically.

MLlib and ML

MLlib and ML are machine learning frameworks that have also been developed by the Spark community. They are included in the Spark source code. You can see the algorithms implemented in MLlib (`https://spark.apache.org/docs/latest/mllib-guide.html`). ML was developed as the sophisticated interface version of MLlib mainly built on top of RDD. Although ML is a newer framework, there is no plan to replace MLlib and make it obsolete. Therefore we do not need to hesitate to keep using MLlib. As described previously, it is very useful to use a training model with the DataFrame API, because it hides the complexity of the interface differences for each problem. ML provides this functionality in a simple way without losing scalability. So the differences between the two frameworks are:

- MLlib provides the original API built on top of RDDs.
- ML provides the higher-level API built on top of DataFrames.

ML also provides the interface for constructing ML pipelines. In machine learning use cases, the preprocessing of data is a critical phase for good accuracy. Ordinal data often has noise that distorts the accuracy of the trained model and a format that is different from the desired ones. Therefore, it is necessary to do preprocessing before passing this data to a training algorithm. But it is usually tough work, even though it is noncore development. The pipeline interface is made for it. This was developed to solve these problems to make the time of the cycle of validation of model shorter. The concept of ML is written in (`https://spark.apache.org/docs/latest/ml-guide.html`). Pipeline provides some kind of components. The important ones are below.

- **Transformer**—transforms one DataFrame into another DataFrame. For example, HashingTF transforms the string into the map based on terms frequency, which contains their term frequency. This `Transformer` may be used in natural language processing, and also machine learning models are categorized into `Transformer`.
- **Estimator**—These are core training algorithms that can be fit on a given DataFrame to produce the `Transformer`. In this case, `Transformer` is a machine learning model that can be used for predicting. `Estimator` is used for training to create a proper machine learning model.
- **Pipeline**—A pipeline contains multiple Transformers and Estimators together in order to specify a machine learning workflow. This component

specifies a sequence of preprocessing units and automatically keeps the sequence for a prediction stage with a trained model.

- **Parameters**—All Transformers and Estimators contain a common API for specifying parameters. You can specify various types of parameters. (e.g., double, int, string).

A pipeline is specified as a sequence of stages. Each stage is composed of a `Transformer` or an `Estimator`. `Transformer#transform` and `Estimator#fit` are called through a training process. So, if you want to use a custom `Transformer`, it is necessary to implement your own `Transformer`, which can override the `transform` method. The illustration of the training process is described below.

In order to create this pipeline, the code snippet can look like this:

```
import org.apache.spark.ml.classification.LogisticRegression
import org.apache.spark.ml.param.ParamMap
import org.apache.spark.mllib.linalg.{Vector, Vectors}
import org.apache.spark.sql.Row
val pipeline = new Pipeline()
        .setStages(Array(tokenizer, hashingTF, logRegression))
```

Pipeline also implements the `fit` method. So you can call the `fit` method when training the model. In this code, `tokenizer` and `hashingTF` are `Transformers`. `logRegression` is the object of `Estimator`. The detail of each class will be described next. The template pattern for creating Pipeline is to put several `Transformers` as a preprocessing component before `Estimator` that is a core machine learning algorithm (e.g., Logistic Regression, Random Forest, etc.).

The important part of the ML Pipeline is that you can easily make use of the scalability of preprocessing components that were developed by the Spark community. Each `Transformer` receives a DataFrame and makes an output as a DataFrame. Usually, the input column name and output column name should be specified as an argument. Here is the list of `Transformers` that might be used in many cases.

`Tokenizer`, `RegexTokenizer`: This `Transformer` can be used as a simple morphological analysis tool for text processing. All input must be some type of feature vector in order to train a machine learning model. The sequence of terms would be converted into the list of terms through splitting with given rules. `Tokenizer` splits the text by white space characters. `RegexTokenizer` splits the text by a given regular expression pattern:

```
val tokenizer = new Tokenizer()
        .setInputCol("sentence").setOutputCol("words")
val regexTokenizer = new RegexTokenizer()
        .setInputCol("sentence").setOutputCol("words")
        .setPattern(",") // Tokenize csv like format
```

`HashingTF`—This converts the list of terms into a fixed length feature vector, which represents the bag-of-words model. This feature vector is a histogram of each term included in a given text. In other words, this transformer counts each terms appearances. So if the given text is "a b c b d c" the output would be [1, 2, 2, 1], and each index corresponds to each term. When you want to use text as an input of the machine learning model, `HashingTF` might be the normal and easiest way:

```
val hashingTF = new HashingTF()
        .setInputCol("words").setOutputCol("features")
```

`StringIndexer`—This `Transformer` can be used for converting the label side. In the context of a classification problem, the labels are discrete values, even represented as strings. But they have to be converted into numeric values when training. `StringIndexer` can do that.

```
val df = sqlContext.createDataFrame( ↵
        Seq((0, "A"), (1, "B"), (2, "C"), (3, "A"), ↵
            (4, "A"), (5, "C"))).toDF("id", "category")
val indexer = new StringIndexer().setInputCol("category") ↵
        .setOutputCol("categoryIndex")
// Add discrete index as categoryIndex column
```

`VectorAsssembler`—When we use DataFrame, there are some cases in which each column represents one element of a given feature. It is necessary to assemble these column values into one feature vector to pass the machine learning model. `VectorAssembler` enables you to do it:

```
val dataset = sqlContext.createDataFrame( ↵
        Seq((0, 25, 2.0, Vectors.dense(0.0, 10.0, 0.5), 1.0)))
            .toDF("userid", "age", "addressCode", ↵
                "userFeatures", "admission")
val vectorAssembler = new VectorAssembler() ↵
        .setInputCols(Array("age", "userFeatures"))
        .setOutputCol("features")
```

You can use the `features` column as an input feature of the machine learning model. Of course there are a lot of `Transformers` that are useful for feature engineering required by all machine learning training processes. Once the feature and label is fixed, you can select the machine learning model and tune it. For tuning, the grid search method can be often used as described in the following paragraphs. This is the role of `Estimators`.

Next, it's time to set up `Estimator` for training. `Estimators` do not return DataFrame when they receive DataFrame. They create a `Model` that can predict the answer you desire. `Model` is similar to the `Transformer`, which was introduced previously. For example, `DecisionTreeClassifier` creates `DecisionTreeClassifierModel` when training is finished.

`DecisionTreeClassifier`—Decision tree is a simple and easy to use algorithm that can be applied to both classification problems and regression problems. Ensemble algorithms for decision tree classifiers have a good performance on the various types of problems. So we can say this is the first algorithm you should try on the real problem. `DecisionTreeClassifier` takes two columns, labels and features. These columns can be set with `setInputCol` and `setOutputCol`. Default values are "label" and "features." So, let's look at the code of the training phase of this classifier through the Pipeline API.

```
val dt = new DecisionTreeClassifier() ↵
      .setLabelCol("label").setFeaturesCol("features")
val pipeline = new Pipeline() ↵
      .setStages(Array(firstTransformer, secondTransformer, dt)
// Returned value is DecisionTreeClassfierModel
val model = pipeline.fit(dataframe)
```

At last we get a model. Then we can continue to the evaluation phase. Every `Model` returned from an `Estimator` has a `transform` method just like `Transformer`. In the evaluation phase, we can combine the method and `Evaluator`. First, we set up a predicted DataFrame.

```
val predictions = model.tranform(testData)
```

`predictions` has a new column named "predictedLabel." This is expected to be the same as the "label" column. This predicted label column name can be changed by using the other `Transformer` at the end of this pipeline. When your problem is a multiple class classification, you can use `MulticlassClassificationEvaluator` to evaluate the prediction of this model.

```
val evaluator = new MulticlassClassificationEvaluator()
      .setLabelCol("label").setPredictionCol("prediction")
      .setMetricName("precision")
```

The metrics can be calculated by comparing the original label and the predicted label according to the given metrics type. There are five types of metrics we can select here that are the same as the ones of the pattern recognition and machine learning terminology:

We introduce three of them because "weightedPrecision" and "weightedRecall are essentially the same as "precision" and "recall" respectively.

- **precision**—Precision is the fraction of the elements labeled properly in all selected elements. This is a simple value often used as accuracy for models.

- **recall**—Recall is the fraction of the elements labeled as positive in all positive elements.

▪ **f1**—This value is calculated for balancing the above two values in order to obtain accuracy. This is the default value of `MulticlassClassificationEvaluator`.

Although there might not be so many cases, you should change this metric type using `Evaluator`; it is highly recommended to evaluate your model after training in some way. The most simple and effective way in the Spark ML package is a grid search with cross validation. Each model has predefined parameters that are not trained through the training process.

For example, let's take a look at `DecisionTreeClassifier` introduced previously. This classifier has `impurity`, `maxBins`, `minInfoGains`, `thresholds`, etc. These are called hyperparameters of the model. They have some degree of freedom. How can we set the nicest values in advance? Cross validation and grid search are the ways for solving this problem. You can use `CrossValidator` when running cross validation. This class receives an `Estimator` that is the target of model selection, a set of parameter maps from which hyper parameters are chosen, and `Evaluators` used to calculate the performance of each model. The code to make cross validation logic looks like this (see Table 6-1):

```
val paramGrid = new ParamGridBuilder()
        .addGrid(dt.impurity, Array("entropy", "gini"))
        .addGrid(dt.minInfoGain, Array(1, 10, 100)).build()
```

Table 6-1: Cross Validation Logic

	ENTROPY	GINI
1	(1, "entropy")	(1, "gini")
10	(10, "entropy")	(10, "gini")
100	(100, "entropy")	(100, "gini")

With this code, we can create a search space that has 6 (2 * 3) combinations. The whole combination pattern is described in Figure 6-2. As you know, it might be difficult to execute an evaluation against all patterns if the number of parameters is increasing. This is because the pattern of possible combinations of parameters is a multiplication of the pattern of each parameter.

`CrossValidator` tries to train models and evaluate on each hyper-parameter candidate combination by using given `Estimator` and `Evaluator`. In other words, the training and evaluation process are done on each cell of Figure 6-2.

```
val cv = new CrossValidator().setEstimator(pipeline)
        .setEvaluator(new MultiClassificationEvaluator)
        .setEstimatorParamMaps(paramGrid).setNumFolds(3)
```

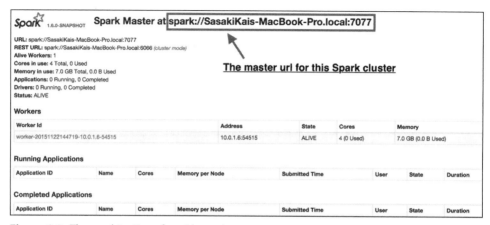

Figure 6-2: The combination of a grid search

numFolds is used to decide the number of folds of cross validation. In this example, the training data is randomly subsampled into three partitions. Only one partition would be used as a validation data set that is used to evaluate the model. And the remaining three partitions are used for a training model. By using the cross validation method, you can use a few data efficiently for training, because we can run the training process k times if separating datasets into k-fold. It is necessary to evaluate and refine your model on procession use cases. This is the general way to do that. After creating the evaluator, you can train the model through the whole Pipeline in the same way.

```
val model = cv.fit(datasets)
```

You can get a refined model including hyper parameters, and a model to predict new coming datasets. We can reduce the possibility of overfitting to training datasets. This is a process to train a machine learning algorithm in the ML Pipeline. Besides this, there are already a lot of algorithms in ML. Of course you can implement your own algorithm within the ML interface. A new algorithm has to implement the Estimator interface first in order to make use of the ML pipeline's sophisticated interface and to keep interoperability.

Mahout on Spark

Apache Mahout is a machine learning library run on the Hadoop framework that was developed relatively early from the stage of distributed machine learning in comparison to other frameworks. Initially, Mahout supported the MapReduce framework as a distributed platform. Then, since other frameworks are more suited for iterative calculations such as machine learning, Mahout was also supporting various kinds of frameworks. Of course Spark is included in this support area. From 0.10, Mahout included a new feature called "Samsara." This is a new mathematic environment for Scala/Spark. Samsara is a linear algebra library written in Scala. On Mahout Samsara, you can write a mathematical calculation in simple Scala DSL. For example, the multiplication of two matrixes such as A and B can be written like `A %*% B`. This calculation can be distributed across the Spark cluster. Mahout Samsara also supports H2O, which is introduced later in this section. H2O is also a distributed machine learning framework that is actively being developed. Let's get started using Mahout on Spark.

Mahout prepares a shell tool that becomes an interface to `spark-shell`. At the beginning, it is necessary to prepare the Spark cluster. One thing to note here is that Mahout `spark-shell` can't handle the Spark local process that is specified by `—master=local[K]`. You need to launch a Spark cluster regardless of the resource manager (YARN, Mesos, etc.), even in local. So as a tutorial, launching a local standalone cluster is the easiest way, because launching a script is already included in the Spark package.

```
$ cd $SPARK_HOME
# Launch Spark standalone cluster on local machine
# It requires administrative privileges
$ ./sbin/start-all.sh
```

You can check that your cluster is launched properly by viewing the web UI. As a default, the Spark UI is hosting the 8080 port on the localhost. Please access `http://localhost:8080/`. The master URL that is necessary to access this cluster is written above in the UI. This URL must be set in the MASTER environment variable in order to access this cluster from the Mahout `spark-shell`. In addition, `SPARK_HOME` and `MAHOUT_HOME` are also necessary to adding dependent classes:

```
$ export SPARK_HOME=/path/to/spark/directory
$ export MAHOUT_HOME=/path/to/mahout/directory
# Set the url that you found on Spark UI
$ export MASTER=spark://XXXXXX:7077
```

That's the preparation for launching the Mahout `spark-shell`. The Mahout command implemented several sub commands and the `spark-shell` sub command is one of them.

```
$ cd $MAHOUT_HOME
$ bin/mahout spark-shell
......
Created spark context..
Spark context is available as "val sc".
Mahout distributed context is available as "implicit val sdc".
SQL context available as "val sqlContext".
mahout>
```

The Mahout `spark-shell` receives Mahout's linear algebra DSL that looks like Scala. The reference of the DSL is written here: `https://mahout.apache.org/users/environment/out-of-core-reference.html`. One unique characteristic given by using the DSL is how Mahout can automatically optimize the parallelism and operations on a distributed raw matrix (DRM), even on Apache Spark. You don't need to recognize what the number of parallelism is or partition tuning that Spark provides. The DSL is often a hard thing to learn, and you have to pay an initial learning cost. But if you keep running your machine learning algorithms on Mahout, mastering this language will pay off due to its optimization and tuning.

Hivemall on Spark

Hivemall is a scalable machine learning framework running on Hive. This framework is implemented as Hive UDF (and also UDTF); therefore, you can run Hivemall on Spark. Hive can be run on several query execution engines such as MapReduce and Tez. With `https://issues.apache.org/jira/browse/HIVE-7292`, Hive can be run on Spark. This means Hivemall can be run on Spark too. Hivemall does not support Spark natively, but the community member implements a wrapper library for Spark.

```
https://github.com/maropu/hivemall-spark
```

The main characteristic of Hivemall is that it has the declarative interface by using SQL(HiveQL) when you want to train a machine learning model or perform other preprocessing. This is also true of hivemall-spark. All you need is a dependency to use hivemall-spark on your environment as a Spark build with Hive or download it from `http://spark.apache.org/downloads.html` (pre-built for Hadoop 2.3 or later). If you want to use the Hive package built by yourself, attach the Hive profile:

```
$ build/mvn -Phive -Pyarn -Phadoop-2.6 \
        -Dhadoop.version=2.6.0 -DskipTests clean package
```

hivemall-spark is published as a Spark package. Therefore, when you launch `spark-shell` or submit your spark jobs with `spark-submit`, you can download hivemall-spark JARs with only adding the —packages options like this:

```
$ $SPARK_HOME/bin/spark-shell \
        —packages maropu:hivemall-spark:0.0.5
```

After that, it is necessary to define UDF references with Hive DDLs. There are a lot of UDFs available in Hivemall. The script to define these UDFs in the Spark context is written in the hivemall-spark repository as `scripts/ddl/define-udfs.sh`.

```
scala> :load define-udfs.sh
```

Using the above command, all UDFs available for Hivemall can also be used in SparkContext. The usage of these algorithms is the same as the original Hivemall. The most important merit of using Hivemall on Spark is DataFrame. You can train Hivemall algorithms with the existing DataFrame like this:

```
val model = sqlContext.createDataFrame(dataset)
        .train_logregr(add_bias($"features"), $"label")
        .groupby("feature").agg("weight", "avg")
        .as("feature", "weight")
```

In addition to this, you can make use of streaming data by combining hive-mall-spark and Spark streaming. This is a unique characteristic because Hive cannot handle streaming data in it alone. In recent years, the requirements and application for streaming data is increasing. hivemall-spark is an option you can choose to run your own production cluster.

External Frameworks

The Spark community provides a lot of frameworks and libraries. The scale and number is growing more and more. In this section, we will introduce various types of external frameworks that are not included in the Spark core source repository. Since the problems Spark is trying to solve cover a lot of fields, these frameworks will reduce the cost of initial development and make use of the knowledge other developers have.

Spark Package

The first thing you have to know to use Spark libraries is Spark packages. This is something like a package manager for Spark. You can download any pack-ages hosted in the Spark package site when you submit a job to a Spark cluster. All packages are hosted on this site.

```
http://spark-packages.org/
```

When you want to use a Spark package, you can add the packages option to the spark-submit command or to the spark-shell command.

```
$ $SPARK_HOME/bin/spark-shell \
        —packages com.databricks:spark-avro_2.10:2.0.1
```

By using the —packages options, Spark packages automatically add the JARs of this package under your classpath. Not only can you use community libraries on your Spark cluster, but you can publish your own library in public. Currently these are the requirements to publish a Spark package into this hosting service:

- The source code must be hosted by GitHub.

- The repository name must be the same as the package name.

- The master branch of the repository must contain the "README.md" and "LICENSE" files under the root directory.

To put it in a different way, you don't need to even build your Spark package. Even if you use the template for the Spark package, building, publishing and versioning will be done by this service. The sbt-spark-package (https://github.com/databricks/sbt-spark-package) plugin for sbt might be useful for generating a Spark package. To include this plugin into your project, please write the below code in your project/plugins.sbt in your sbt project.

```
resolvers += "bintray-spark-packages" at "https://dl.bintray.com/ ↵
spark-packages/maven/"
    addSbtPlugin("org.spark-packages" % "sbt-spark-package" % "0.2.3")
```

The required information to publish the Spark package is below. These should be written in build.sbt:

- spName—The name of your Spark package.

- sparkVersion—The Spark version on which your package depends.

- sparkComponents—The list of dependencies in Spark components on which your package depends such as SQL, MLlib.

- spShortDescription—One line description of your package.

- spDescription—Full description of your package.

- spHomepage—The URL of the web page which describes your package.

The six items described above are the only thing that you should write before pushing. Be sure to push the master branch of your package repository. You can follow the WebUI of a Spark package hosting site (http://spark-packages.org/), as shown in Figure 6-3.

After registering the Spark package site with your GitHub account, you can select your repository from the pull down menu named "name" (see Figure 6-4). The short description and homepage might be better as the same description and homepage URL of the ones written in build.sbt. Once you submit your package, the verification process starts. The verification usually takes a few minutes to complete. You'll receive an email when the verification is finished, telling you if it was successful or not. If successful, your package can be downloaded using the —package option as described earlier. The Spark package site hosts 153 total packages as of November, 2015. The libraries that will be introduced in the next sections also support the Spark package, which means they will also be distributed in the Spark package format.

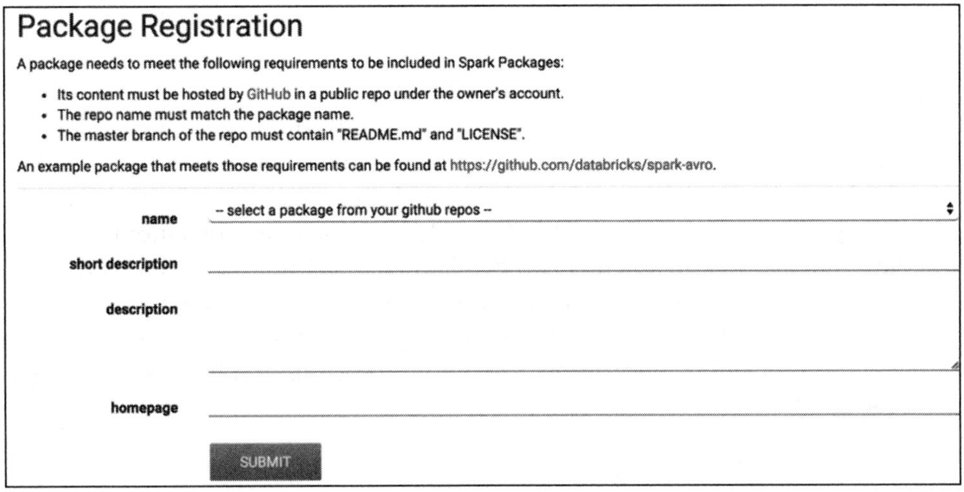

Package Registration

A package needs to meet the following requirements to be included in Spark Packages:

- Its content must be hosted by GitHub in a public repo under the owner's account.
- The repo name must match the package name.
- The master branch of the repo must contain "README.md" and "LICENSE".

An example package that meets those requirements can be found at https://github.com/databricks/spark-avro.

name	– select a package from your github repos –
short description	
description	
homepage	

SUBMIT

Figure 6-3: The package registration site

Packages and releases submitted for verification:

type	name	user	create time	updated time	state	message
release	Lewuathe/spark-kaggle-examples:0.0.1	Lewuathe	2015-11-22 03:23:01	2015-11-22 03:23:01	pending	Please check again later.

Figure 6-4: Selecting a package name

XGBoost

XGBoost is an optimization library used especially for distributed frameworks. This framework is developed by the DMLC (Distributed Machine Learning Common). As its name suggests, there are many machine learning libraries that also have a high-scalability running on existing resources such as Hadoop and Spark under the DMLC project. XGBoost is based on the algorithm called gradient boosting. The Tree boosting algorithm is a kind of ensemble learning for classification that is combining a decision tree and boosting algorithm. This is a lightweight and fast classification algorithm. Although the explanation of the detail tree ensemble and tree boosting algorithms are omitted here, they are simple and efficient algorithms: `https://xgboost.readthedocs.org/en/latest/model.html`.

Although currently XGBoost cannot be integrated with Spark, a lot of reputations around XGBoost brought the Spark community to develop the Spark package for XGBoost: `http://spark-packages.org/package/rotationsymmetry/sparkxgboost/`.

Although this package does not seem to be supported by the core team of XGBoost, you can try the implementation of XGBoost on Spark by using the `sparkxgboost` package.

spark-jobserver

Submitting jobs needs improvement because it is a little difficult for nonengineers. You need to understand how to use the command line or some UNIX commands to submit Spark jobs. A current submitting tool prepared by the Spark project is the CLI. spark-jobserver provides a RESTful API for managing jobs submitted into the Spark cluster. So this means you can launch Spark as a service inside your in-house enterprise environment. The easiest tutorial for using spark-observer is launching a Docker container, which is prepared by their developers. If you already have a Docker environment on your laptop, all you have to do is type this command:

```
$ docker run -d -p 8090:8090 \
        velvia/spark-jobserver:0.5.2-SNAPSHOT
```

With this command, the Docker image for spark-jobserver will be downloaded, which will launch spark-jobserver on Docker as a daemon process. You can see this server status with port 8090. After launching you see the web UI like that shown in Figure 6-5. This is simple, but it does provide sufficient information to manage your job. The backend of the job server is a Spark cluster with a local executor that has four threads that are running under this Docker container configuration, though this might not be sufficient for your production use case. So, let's suppose your job is sent through a REST API. A famous word count example is included in the spark-jobserver project directory. After downloading the source code, build it using the `sbt` command. If you don't have `sbt` yet installed on your laptop, please refer to: `http://www.scala-sbt.org/`.

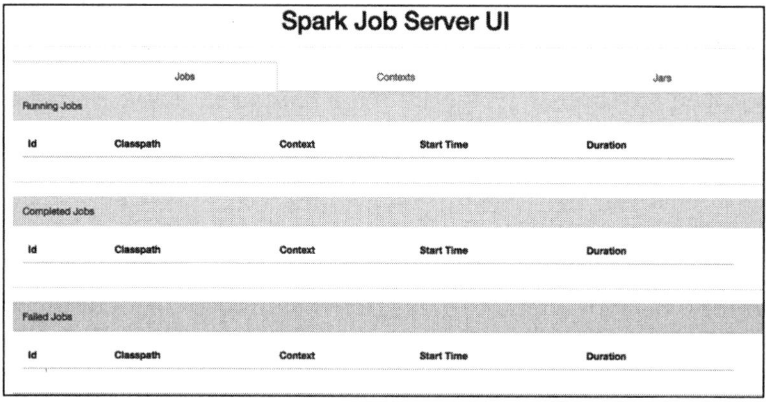

Figure 6-5: The Spark Job Server UI

```
$ git clone \
      https://github.com/spark-jobserver/spark-jobserver.git
$ cd spark-jobserver
$ sbt job-server-tests/package
# You can get build test package as a jar format under
# job-server-tests/target/scala-2.10/job-server-
# tests_2.10-0.6.1-SNAPSHOT.jar, though version number
# might be a little bit different.
```

The process of running a job is 1) to upload the JAR file of your application, and 2) to select the main class to be run on spark-jobserver. It is unnecessary to write the Spark application or build it every time you want to submit the job, even if you want to share it with other members. The spark-jobserver persists:

- Job status

- Job configuration

- Jars

So, once you set this information, you don't need to re-upload it. More than anything, you can share your application code with your colleagues on spark-jobserver. You can upload using the curl command:

```
$ curl --data-binary @job-server-tests/target/scala-2.10/job-server- ↵
tests_2.10-0.6.1-SNAPSHOT.jar \
    http://<Your Docker Host IP>:8090/jars/test
$ curl 'http://<Your Docker Host IP>:8090/jars'
    {
      "tests": "2015-11-12T02:26:50.069-05:00"
    }
```

It is okay to upload your JAR file if you receive the message above. It's time to start your application with the input data.

```
$ curl -d "input.string = takeshi nobita dora suneo suneo nobita" ' ↵
http://<Your Docker Host IP>:8090/jobs?appName=tests&classPath=spark. ↵
jobserver.WordCountExample'
$ curl 'http://<Your Docker Host IP>:8090/jobs'
    {
      "duration": "0.448 secs",
      "classPath": "spark.jobserver.WordCountExample",
      "startTime": "2015-11-12T03:01:12.362-05:00",
      "context": "0a518c58-spark.jobserver.WordCountExample",
      "status": "FINISHED",
      "jobId": "aed9a387-5319-4d8e-ac3d-0f1ce9d4b1a1"
    }
```

Your job should be finished and successful. The result can also be downloaded through a REST API:

```
$ curl http://<Your Docker Host IP>:8090/jobs/aed9a387-5319-4d8e- ⏎
ac3d-0f1ce9d4b1a1
    {
      "status": "OK",
      "result": {
        "takeshi": 1,
        "nobita": 2,
        "suneo": 2,
        "dora": 1
      }
    }
```

This is one process for using spark-jobserver. Although this library is actively under development, it may soon work in practical use cases because it is an open source project. If you are considering the in-house usage for daily data processing, spark-jobserver might be a nice option.

Future Works

You may be interested in using Spark on your service. Spark is already providing a lot of functionality, such as SQL execution, streaming processing, and machine learning. Spark also has an easy-to-use interface. Spark is actively being developed by a powerful community, which may be why people have high expectations for Spark. Here we will cover some Spark projects that are currently in progress.

The main data structures that Spark currently uses are RDD and DataFrame. RDD was an initial concept, and DataFrame was introduced later. RDD is relatively flexible. You can run many types of transformations and calculations against RDD structures. However, due to this flexibility, it's hard to optimize its executions. On the other hand, DataFrame has a somewhat fixed structure and this characteristic enables you to optimize executions on DataFrame datasets. But, it lacks the advantages that RDD has, primarily its flexibility. The main difference between RDD and DataFrame is described in Table 6-2.

Table 6-2: The Difference between RDD and DataFrame

RDD	DATAFRAME
Type safety (Compile time)	Saving memory usage
A lot of codes and users	Faster sort/serialization
Easy to write adhoc logic	Logical IR for optimization

The Spark Dataset API aims to provide a way to write transformation code easily for users and achieve a nice performance and robustness at the same time under a type-safe mechanism.

The goals of the Dataset API are:

- The performance of the Dataset API should be equal to or better than the existing RDD API. The processing and serialization speed should be **faster** than existing APIs.

- Like RDDs, the Dataset API should provide compile time *type-safety*. The scheme should be known at compile time if possible. It enables you to do fail-fast development when there is some mismatch on scheme in terms of the level of type system.

- Support for various types of object models, such as primitive types, case classes, tuples, and JavaBeans.

- The Dataset API can be used with both Scala and Java. When shared types cannot be used, overloaded functions will be provided to both languages.

- The Dataset API should have interoperability with the DataFrame API. Users should transition seemlessly between the Dataset API and the DataFrame. Libraries such as MLlib should not need to implement different interfaces for the Dataset and DataFrame.

The initial image of usage for the Dataset API is similar to the following snippet according to the current design:

```
val ds: Dataset[Int] = Seq(1, 2, 3, 4, 5).toDS()
val ds2: Dataset[Pair[Int, Long]]
        = ds.groupBy(_ % 2).countByKey()
```

Existing data (such as Collections) can be encoded into the Dataset easily. But note that this has not yet been released. The possibility of a changing design of the API is reasonably high. The discussion and development of the Dataset API is progressing under SPARK-9999 JIRA. The latest information about it will appear on the ticket (SPARK-9999).

Integration with the Parameter Server

Before introducing the implementations of the parameter server, it is necessary to clarify the concept of distributed machine learning, i.e., Parallelism. Understanding the background and difficulties of large scale machine learning may help you know the purpose of developing the parameter server. They are not a system of simple key-value stores such as Redis or Cassandra. The goal of the parameter server is different from existing databases. They are developed for large scale machine learning. There are two types of parallelism in large scale distributed machine learning: data parallelism and model parallelism. These concepts are a little complicated and the differences are not well known. So let's tackle them one at a time.

Data Parallelism

Data parallelism focuses on distributing the data across the different computing resources inside the cluster. Usually, the training data for machine learning is huge. Only one node machine cannot keep all of that data on memory, or sometimes even in the disk. This is a type of SIMD processing. All processors (or machines) perform the same tasks on different data. In the context of machine learning, training processes run on each data split kept in each machine. So if there are 10 machines, you can run 10 training processes. But at the same time 10 models are given to you in spite of only one model being necessary. Each training process generates different models. These are 10. How can it consolidate these 10 trained models into one? The easiest way is to calculate the average of these models. Taking an average of each parameter of a model provides a relatively good performance.

Most of the distributed machine learning frameworks including Spark MLlib and ML implement data parallelism. Although data parallelism is simple and easy to implement, the collecting task (in the previous case a calculation of average) of data parallelism can bottleneck, because this task must wait for other parallel tasks distributed among the cluster. Data parallelism (see Figure 6-6) produces multiple models on each training iterations. In order to use this trained model properly, it is necessary to create one model based on these multiple models.

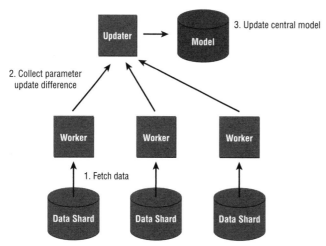

Figure 6-6: Data parallelism

Model Parallelism

Model parallelism is something quite different from data parallelism. Different machines train with the same data. However, a model is distributed across multiple machines. A model of deep learning tends to become so huge because a lot of parameters are not always on a single machine. Model parallelism is the concept of splitting a single model into several parts. One node keeps a part of the whole model. On the other hand, each training process can update a model asynchronously. This must be managed by a framework in order to keep consistency of the model. The frameworks that realize it, especially for machine learning, are called the "Parameter Servers." Model parallelism is required especially for deep learning because deep learning requires more data, shown in Figure 6-7, and eventually it means more parameters. The model cannot be on one machine, and disk and memory. So if we have to try deep learning, it is indispensable to use a parameter server in your production cluster.

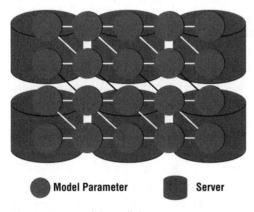

Model Parameter   **Server**

Figure 6-7: Model parallelism

A model is managed by multiple servers under model parallelism. Thanks to this, we can manipulate a huge model that cannot be stored on one machine. A machine in this cluster only keeps a part of the whole model. The complete model can be reconstructed by combining all parts stored in this cluster. This is tough work if you have to manage the health check of each fragmentation and construct the complete model in a specific way. That's the reason why the parameter server exists. Parameter servers are often similar to NoSQL data storage. Redis, MongoDB, and Cassandra are examples. The unique characteristics of parameter servers are 1) focusing on updating the data in a distributed way, and 2) keeping complete data as a whole within the cluster. This concept is pretty new and not adapted by many companies. But this is one of the most important technologies to run large scale machine learning algorithms and keep its models. In the next section, some implementations of the parameter server will be introduced. They may not be easy to use in their current phase. It will be good for you to grasp the whole image and architecture of each implementation.

Parameter Server and Spark

As described previously, the original parameter server is developed for model parallel processing. Most algorithms in Spark MLlib currently process data under the concept of data parallel, but not model parallelism. In order to realize the model parallel in a general way, the architecture of the parameter server is studied and developed for more efficiency. The parameter server holds and updates a model in the distributed cluster on RAM. Updating the mode often becomes the bottleneck in the distributed learning process. SPARK-6932 is a ticket for investigating the potential of the parameter server and a comparison between each implementation. Moreover, the Spark project is trying to implement its own "parameter server" based on the investigation. The parameter server on Spark was already provided, `https://github` `.com/chouqin/spark/tree/ps-on-spark-1.3`, though this is still under discussion because it requires some change of the core source code. In addition to this, there are several implementations of the parameter server. Yet, this software is not adapted to developers and enterprise broadly. It might be helpful to know what products there are and what characteristics each implementation has in order to catch up with the trend of using scalable machine learning services.

CMU Machine Learning

DMLC implements XGBoost as described previously, and also develops a type of parameter server. This implements the Chord hashing table in order to make it easy to synchronize the entire data. In production use cases, all servers can be broken and can fail. Distributed systems such as Hadoop HDFS, YARN, and Spark must have a high fault tolerance. The parameter server can be also the key component in terms of machine learning with these types of distributed systems. The CMU parameter server implements the Chord style algorithm for fault tolerance.

If you want to try the DMLC parameter server, you have to build your own binary. It is recommended to build on Ubuntu (or another Linux distribution). You cannot build the parameter server on Mac OS X at the time of this writing. After preparing your own Ubuntu machine, you need to install some dependencies:

```
$ sudo apt-get update && \
      sudo apt-get install -y build-essential git
```

Download the source code and build it.

```
$ git clone https://github.com/dmlc/ps-lite
$ cd ps-lite && make deps -j4 && make -j4
```

You will see the example code under the `build` directory. It might be good to run some examples in order to grasp the whole process of how the parameter server works. So let's run `example_a` and `example_b`, according to a tutorial. There are two APIs to understand how the parameter server works at the first step: push and pull. The Push API is used to update parameters stored in the parameter server. Pull is used for referencing that parameter value. Generally speaking, at the end of the iteration of the training process, the Push API is used for updating the model parameter. At the beginning of each iteration, the process fetches all of the parameters to reconstruct the parameter server on its memory. This whole process can be achieved asynchronously and reliably by using the parameter server without losing scalability. The code snippet that indicates how we can do this is shown here:

```
typedef float Val
// Define key indicators that must be
// unsigned integer type currently
std::vector<Key> keys = {1, 2, 3};
std::vector<Val> values = {1, 10, 20};
// Worker process is the client that manipulates
// stored data in parameter server.
KVWorker<Val> worker;
// Update values corresponding keys
int ts = wk.Push(keys, values);
// Wait the ack from parameter server
wk.wait(ts);
```

With this code, you can update the parameters stored in the parameter server. Next, you can pull the API to fetch these stored parameters:

```
// Define the variables stores returned parameter from
// parameter server. They do not have index but sorted.
std::vector<Val> recv_values;
ts = wk.Pull(key, &recv_values);
wk.wait(ts);
example_a writes the tutorial of this pattern. The command to run this ↵
  is here.
$ ./local.sh 1 5 ./example_a
values pulled at W3: [3]: 1 10 20
values pulled at W0: [3]: 2 20 40
values pulled at W2: [3]: 4 40 80
values pulled at W1: [3]: 4 40 80
values pulled at W4: [3]: 5 50 100
```

`local.sh` is a helper script to run the parameter server and workers. The first argument represents the number of the parameter server, and the second one is for the number of worker nodes. Both of them are running a local machine. Although these processes run asynchronously, the result might be a little bit different. In this case, five workers are updating the parameter stored in one parameter server and fetching a parameter list immediately. Every worker does not fetch the value that is applied by its own addition. In the above case, W3 cannot fetch the value [3 30 60], which should have been added just before fetching since the local.sh script launches each worker sequentially. In order to solve this, you can add the dependency into each operation as an option. This dependency means "this operation should be done after each previous push operation is finished." So this worker can see its own value that pushed just before without waiting. You can add this dependency as follows:

```
KVWorker<Val> wk;
int ts = wk.Push(keys, values);
SyncOpts options;
// Set the dependency above pushed data
options.deps = {ts};
// When the dependency is satisfied,
// this function will be called
options.callback = [&recv_values]() {
std::cout << "values pulled at " << MyNodeID() << ": "
Blob<const Val>(recv_values) << std::endl;
};
ts = wk.Pull(keys, &recv_values, options);
wk.Wait(ts);
```

By setting up the above dependency, you are guaranteed to obtain the latest value that is applied to the dependent push operations. Overall, this parameter server API is simple and easy to use. All you have to do is write some C++ code for getting the scalable model for updating the architecture (see Figure 6-8).

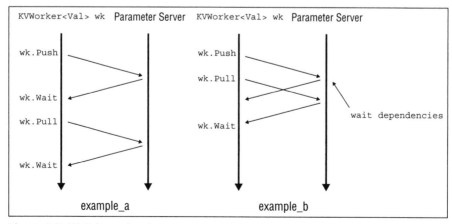

Figure 6-8: Wait dependencies

Google DistBelief

Google DistBelief is an internal system of Google. You can read more about that here: `http://research.google.com/pubs/pub40565.html`. This paper shows you the concept of model parallelism and an overview of large scale machine learning infrastructure used inside Google. DistBelief was used for various applications provided by Google such as speech recognition, image search, and DeepDream that tries to create its own new "image" based on the deep learning algorithm. The team lead by Jeffrey Dean recently open sourced TensorFlow (`http://tensorflow.org/`) that is trying to overcome DistBelief shortcomings. TensorFlow is aimed to calculate general numeric computation, but it currently does not seem to support Spark or Hadoop platforms. So we will omit the detail of TensorFlow here. It might be helpful to learn how to run TensorFlow, because it is a good resource to learn the basic concept and algorithms for deep learning.

Factorbird

Factorbird is a prototype parameter server developed primarily by Stanford University. It improves the scalability of algorithms based on the stochastic gradient descent. Factorbird employs a lock-free shared memory model as a parameter server architecture. This is called Hogwild! style. It is designed to meet the followings points:

- Scalability to tall and wide matrices with dozens of billions of nonzeros.
- Extensibility to different kinds of models and loss functions as long as they can be optimized using SGD.
- Adaptability to both batch and streaming scenarios.

As a reference for the Factorbird parameter server, the paper about Hogwild! is important to read: `https://www.eecs.berkeley.edu/~brecht/papers/hogwildTR.pdf`.

Petuum

Petuum is a distributed machine learning framework, which aims to provide a generic algorithm and interface and simplify the distributed implementation of a machine learning program. Petuum includes an asynchronous distributed key-value store for parallel machine learning. This storage system is called Bösen. Bösen does not seem to work purely asynchronously. This model is defined as a synchronous parallel consistency model. It provides more performance than a complete synchronous model, and it also achieves the model correctness at the same time. Bösen has been already used by Microsoft's distributed ML toolkit (DMTK), which was recently open sourced. So this means that Bösen has actual results in the industrial field, even though it was renamed as multiverse (`https://github.com/Microsoft/multiverso`).

Vowpal Wabbit

Vowpal Wabbit is a machine learning framework researched by Yahoo! and supported by Microsoft. Given how this is now integrated into Microsoft Azure, you can indirectly use this framework.

Project Tungsten

Traditionally, optimizing I/O (network, disk) was always the most effective way to tune performance in a distributed system. I/O has been the most scarce and bottlenecked resource for a long time. Thanks to the progress of hardware and technology about data compression, this is changing. By observing Spark use cases, the Spark community found that the many workloads run on Spark are not bottlenecked by I/O or network, but rather by CPU and memory. Project Tungsten aims to improve the efficiency of memory and CPU for Spark applications. Each application can be restricted by the limit of underlying hardware. It is often called a bottleneck of your system. The main focuses of this project are:

- **Avoiding nontransient Java objects (store them in binary format), which reduces garbage collection (GC) overhead.** The one big thing Tungsten aims to do is to reduce GC. So Tungsten also tries to manage the memory manually by using the Unsafe feature, which was introduced in JDK 1.7. This means that Spark has to manage the off-heap object by itself on behalf of the JVM. The manual memory management can often be a risky way if you don't understand how Spark handles manual memory management safely by using the knowledge of the data schema represented by DataFrame usage. This can also minimize the memory footprint.

- **Minimizing memory usage through improving data format.** By using a dense data format such as Parquet or ORC, you can optimize the usage of memory.

- **Cache-aware Computation for faster sorting and aggregation.** It introduced a new shuffle manager that directly manages memory when doing a shuffle sort called `UnsafeShuffleManager`. This manager can sort serialized binary data, but not Java objects, which can reduce memory consumption and GC overhead.

- **Implement faster serialization/deserialization.** Operators that understand data types can process a binary format directly in memory. This reduces the overhead of serialization/deserialization. It means that Spark operators can handle a binary format that represents DataFrame/Spark SQL data by using the unsafe feature of JVM. It can support not only off-heap data, but also on-heap data. In on-heap mode, however, data is managed by the address of the base Java object and offset within the object. In off-heap mode, each data is addressed with a 64 bit long memory address directly.

In other words, Spark becomes able to fit more of its own CPU intensive workloads. This project is split into two phases according to the project JIRA ticket. The first one has already been finished, released in the 1.5 version. The remaining items in the second phase should be available in the 1.6 version. This includes interface and optimization improvements. Although the Tungsten project is difficult to see for Spark users, it is very important for the future of Spark, providing what will become the next level of distributed computing. Be sure to look for the release of Spark 1.6.

Deep Learning

Deep learning is the most focused area in machine learning because of its high accuracy and generality. This algorithm emerged and won a lot of competitions around 2011-2012. In the beginning, deep learning succeeded with audio and image recognition. In addition to this, natural language processing such as machine translation or drawing pictures can be done using the deep learning algorithm. Deep learning is a type of neural network that has been used for a long time since around 1980. The neural network is regarded as the machine that is able to do universal approximation. In other words, this type of network can mimic any other functions. For example, the deep learning algorithm can create a function for classifying a cat or dog when given animal pictures. Deep learning can be regarded as a deep structure that stacks a lot of neural networks.

As described in the proviso section regarding the parameter server, deep learning requires a lot of parameter and training data compared to other existing machine learning algorithms. That's why we are introducing the deep learning framework that can be run on Spark here. It is indispensable to get a reliable and fast distributed engine for stable deep learning training in an enterprise environment. Spark is seen currently as one of the most suitable platforms for deep learning because

1) on-memory processing architecture is fit for iterative calculations that use machine learning algorithms, especially deep learning, and

2) Spark has several ecosystems useful for developing deep learning models such as MLlib and Tachyon.

In the last section of this chapter, we'll introduce some deep learning frameworks that can be used with Spark. These frameworks are relatively new libraries as is deep learning itself. It is possible that you may encounter some bugs or lack of operation tools by using them, but reporting issues and sending patches will help take care of that.

H2O

H2O is a scalable machine learning framework developed by H2O.ai, and it isn't restricted to deep learning. H2O supports a lot of APIs (e.g., R, Python, Scala and Java). Of course this is open source software, therefore you can easily investigate the codes and algorithms. The H2O framework supports all common databases and file types. You can easily export the model into a lot of types of storages. The deep learning algorithms are implemented in another library called spar-kling-water (`http://h2o.ai/product/sparkling-water/`). This is developed mainly by h2o.ai. In order to run sparkling-water, Spark 1.3 or later is necessary.

Installation

1. First you can download the latest sparkling-water from the h2o site.

    ```
    http://h2o-release.s3.amazonaws.com/sparkling-water/rel-1.3/1/index
    .html
    ```

2. Point it to your Spark installation directory:

    ```
    $ export SPARK_HOME=/path/to/your/spark/
    ```

3. You can launch `sparkling-shell`, which is an interface like `spark-shell`:

    ```
    $ cd ~/Downloads
    $ unzip sparkling-water-1.3.1.zip
    $ cd sparkling-water-1.3.1
    $ bin/sparkling-shell
    ```

There are several examples included in the sparkling-water source code repository. Unfortunately some of the examples don't work correctly with the latest Spark (1.5.2). The deep learning demo has the same problem. You will have to wait or contribute some patches to be run on Spark.

deeplearning4j

deeplearning4j is developed by Skymind, a company that aims to commercial-ize deep learning for the enterprise. This framework was created to run on Hadoop and Spark. It was designed to be used in business environments rather than in a research field where there are many deep learning frameworks and libraries in use. Skymind is the main supporter, but this is open source software, and they welcome any patches from you. The implemented algorithms in this framework are as follows:

- Restricted Boltzmann machine
- Convolutional Neural network
- Recurrent Neural network
- Recursive autoencoder
- Deep-Belief network
- Deep autoencoder
- Stacked denoising autoencoder

The great thing to note here is that these models can be configured at a fine-grained level. You can set the number of hidden layers, the activation function of each neural as you like, and the number of iterations. deeplearning4j provides various types of network implementations and flexible model parameters. Skymind is also developing a lot of tools that are useful for running machine learning more reliably. Here are some of them:

- **Canova** (`https://github.com/deeplearning4j/Canoba`) **is a vectorization library.** A machine learning algorithm can only handle all data in a vector format. All pictures, audio, and text data must be converted into vector by using some method. Although it is common work to train the machine learning model, this would be reinventing the wheel and can also cause bugs. Canova can do this conversion for you. The current input data formats supported by Canova are:
  - CSV
  - Raw Text (Tweets, Documents)
  - Image (Pictures, Drawings)
  - Customer file format (such as MNIST)
- **Since Canova is written primarily in Java, it can be run on all JVM platforms.** So you can use it on the Spark cluster as well. Even if you don't do deep learning, Canova may help you with your machine learning tasks.
- **nd4j** (`https://github.com/deeplearning4j/nd4j`) **is like a numpy, SciPy tool in Python.** This tool provides you with scientific computing like linear algebra, vector calculation, and manipulations. This is also written in Java. You can combine these tools to fit in your use case. And the point to note is that nd4j supports GPU functionality. You can expect fast computation since modern computation hardware is progressing.
- **dl4j-spark-ml** (`https://github.com/deeplearning4j/dl4j-spark-ml`) **is a Spark package that enables you to use deeplearning4j easily on**

Spark. By using this package, you can integrate deeplearning4j on Spark with only one-liners, because it has been uploaded in the Spark package public repository (`http://spark-packages.org/package/deeplearning4j/dl4j-spark-ml`).

So we recommend that you use deeplearning4j on Spark by using the dl4j-spark-ml package. As usual, it is necessary to download or build your own Spark source code. In particular, there are no requirements for the Spark version. You can just use the earliest version. The deeplearning4j project has prepared several example repositories. In order to try deeplearning4j on Spark, the dl4j-spark-ml-examples (`https://github.com/deeplearning4j/dl4j-spark-ml-examples`) are the best examples to use. Here you can see how to download and build this repository.

```
$ git clone git@github.com:deeplearning4j/dl4j-spark-mlexamples.git
$ cd dl4j-spark-ml-examples
$ mvn clean package -Dspark.version=1.5.2 \
                    -Dhadoop.version=2.6.0
```

The build classes are positioned under the target directory, but you can run these examples using the `bin/run-example` script. There are currently three types of examples:

- `ml.JavaIrisClassification`—Classification for iris flower data set.

- `ml.JavaLfwClassification`—Classification for LFW face database.

- `ml.JavaMnistClassification`—Classification for MNIST handwriting data.

Let's select the third one, running a training of the classification model for the MNISt handwriting data set. Before running this, it is necessary to download the training data from the MNIST site (`http://yann.lecun.com/exdb/mnist/`). Or you can download it using the following command:

```
## Download hand writing image data
$ wget http://yann.lecun.com/exdb/mnist/train-images-idx3-ubyte.gz
$ gunzip train-images-idx3-ubyte
## Download the labels corresponding to the above images
$ wget http://yann.lecun.com/exdb/mnist/train-labels-idx1-ubyte.gz
$ gunzip train-labels-idx1-ubyte
And then put the two files on data directory under dl4j-spark-ml- ↵
examples.
$ mv train-images-idx3-ubyte \
        /path/to/dl4j-spark-ml-examples/data
$ mv train-labels-idx1-ubyte \
        /path/to/dl4j-spark-ml-examples/data
```

It's almost time to start running the training process. The last thing you have to pay attention to is the memory size of the Spark executor and driver, because the MNIST data set and the training model for that will become huge. It requires a lot of memory, so we recommend that you change the memory size written in the `bin/run-example` script in advance. You can change the last line of the `bin/run-example` script as follows:

```
exec spark-submit \
        --packages "deeplearning4j:dl4j-spark-ml:0.4-rc0" \
        --master $EXAMPLE_MASTER \
        --class $EXAMPLE_CLASS \
        --driver-memory 8G \      # <- Changed from 1G
        --executor-memory 8G \    # <- Changed from 4G
        "$SPARK_EXAMPLES_JAR" \
        "$@"
```

It is now time to start training:

```
$ MASTER=local[4] bin/run-example ml.JavaMnistClassification
```

In order to specify the master configuration of local Spark, we have set the MASTER environment variable before the `bin/run-example` script. This training will take some time, although it depends on your environment and machine specs. This sample runs a type of neural network called the convolutional neural network. The parameter detail is set with the `MultiLayerConfiguration` class. Since deeplearning4j has a Java interface, even if you are not used to Scala in which Spark is written, it might be an easy introduction. Here is a simple explanation of the convolutional neural network parameters for this example:

- `seed`—The neural network uses random variables such as the initial network parameter. This seed is used to generate these parameters. Thanks to this seed argument, it becomes easy to test or debug to develop the machine learning model.

- `batchSize`—The iterative algorithm, such as the gradient descent, sums up some update values before updating the model. batchSize specifies the number of samples on which the update value is calculated.

- `iterations`—The model parameters are kept updated by an iterative process. This parameter decides how many times this iteration is processed. The longer the iteration becomes, the possibility of convergence becomes higher, in general.

- `optimizationAlgo`—There are several methods required to run the iterative process previously described. The stochastic gradient descent (SGD) is a state of the art method that does not relatively fall into the local minimum and can keep searching the global minimum point.

- `layer`—This is a core configuration of the deep learning algorithm. The deep learning neural network has several network groups called **layer**.

This parameter decides what type of layer will be used in each layer. For example, in case of a convolutional neural network, ConvolutionLayer is used to extract features of an input image. This layer can learn what type of characteristics a given picture has. Putting this layer at the beginning, this whole network will improve the accuracy of prediction. Each layer also can be configured with given parameters.

```
new ConvolutionLayer.Builder(10, 10)
              .nIn(nChannels) // The number of input element
              .nOut(6)        // The number of output element
              .weightInit(WeightInit.DISTRIBUTION)
                              // Initialisation method for
              // parameter matrix
              .activation("sigmoid") // Activation function type
              .build())
```

Figure 6-9 shows you the general structure of a neural network. Since ConvolutionalLayer is also a type of neural network, the components of both networks are almost the same. The neural network has an input (*x*) and output (*y*). Both of them are vector format data. In Figure 6-9, the input is a four dimensional vector, and the output is also a four dimensional vector. How can it calculate output vector *y*? Each layer has a parameter matrix, in this case, and they are represented by **W**. The multiplication of *x* and **W** becomes the next vector. In order to enhance the expressiveness of the model, this vector is passed to some nonlinear activation function (σ) such as a logistic sigmoid function, the softmax function. By using this nonlinear function, the neural network can approximate any type of function. And then *z* is multiplied by another parameter matrix **W** and again an activation function σ is applied.

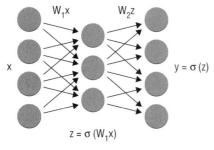

Figure 6-9: Conceptual diagram of a neural network

You can see how each configuration of ConvolutionLayer. nIn and nOut is a dimension of the input vector(*x*) and the output vector(*z*). activation is for the activation function of this layer that can be selected by the logistic sigmoid function, and the rectified linear unit. The dimensions of the input and output can immediately be decided according to your problem. Other parameters should be optimized through grid search, described next.

The selection of each layer is often difficult to decide by ourselves. It requires some knowledge and research of a particular problem that you are trying to solve. The deeplearning4j project also prepares an introductory document (`http://deeplearning4j.org/convolutionalnets.html`). Though it requires a little math and linear algebra, this is one of the easiest documentations that describe how convolutional neural networks work.

- `backprop`—Backpropagation is a state of the art method used to update the model parameter (W). So this parameter should always be true.

- **pretrain**—Thanks to pretraining, the multilayer network can obtain optimized initial parameters for extracting features from input data. It is also recommended to be true.

We cannot describe the whole detail of deep learning here. But generally, these algorithms are all major ones to use for various types of use cases covering image recognition, text processing, and spam-filtering. The official site of deeplearning4j provides not only the usage of deeplearning4j, but also has a general discussion about deep learning. You can also learn the cutting edge technology and concept. Please check it out: `http://deeplearning4j.org/`.

SparkNet

This is the newest library introduced in this book. SparkNet was published Nov 2015 from the AMP lab at UC Berkeley. Spark is also originally developed by the AMP lab. So it is fair to say the "official deep learning library running on Spark." This library provides an interface for reading RDD, and a compatible interface for the Caffe (`http://caffe.berkeleyvision.org/`) deep learning framework. SparkNet achieved a simple parallel scheme by adopting the stochastic gradient descent. SparkNet jobs can be submitted with spark-submit. You can easily use this new library.

The architecture of SparkNet is simple. SparkNet is responsible for the distributed processing, and the core learning process is delegated to the Caffe framework. SparkNet uses Java native access with the C API that is provided by the Caffe framework. Caffe is implemented in C++, and the C wrapper of Caffe is written under the `libcaffe` directory in SparkNet. Therefore the total code base of SparkNet is relatively small. The Java code (`CaffeLibrary.java`) wraps the library moreover. In order to use the `CaffeLibrary` from Scala world, `CaffeNet` is provided. The hierarchy of this is shown in Figure 6-10.

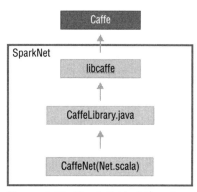

Figure 6-10: The CaffeNet hierarchy

Application developers of SparkNet should only care about `CaffeNet` if you are familiar with Scala. And you can also use Spark RDD. This is also realized making a wrapper called with the `JavaDataLayer` C++ code. In addition to this, SparkNet can load the model file written in the Caffe format. The extension is usually set by `.prototxt`:

```
val netParameter
    = ProtoLoader.loadNetPrototxt(sparkNetHome
        + "your-caffemodel.prototxt")
```

Replacing the input of this model, you can train your own data on Spark. SparkNet also provides this utility.

```
val newNetParameter =
    ProtoLoader.replaceDataLayers(netParameter,
      trainBatchSize, testBatchSize,
      numChannels, height, width)
```

As its name suggests, the meanings of each parameter defines the batch size and input size of each phase (training, test, etc.). The detail of each parameter can be confirmed in the official Caffe document (`http://caffe.berkeleyvision.org/tutorial/net_layer_blob.html`). In other words, by using SparkNet you can easily use Caffe with the Scala language on Spark. If you are already familiar with Caffe, SparkNet might be a tool you can try with ease.

Enterprise Usage

In this last section, we want to explain some of the enterprise practical use cases we have experienced. Although it is often difficult to disclose confidential contents, we want to clarify what Spark can do and what is necessary for making full use of Spark. These are all actual use cases by our companies.

Collecting User Activity Log with Spark and Kafka

Collecting user activity logs contributes to improving the accuracy of recommendation or visualization of effect of each policy that your company took. Hadoop and Hive are mainly used in this field. Hadoop is the only platform that can process huge data like activity logs. Thanks to Hive interface, we could analyze somewhat interactively. But this architecture has three disadvantages.

- Time consuming analysis by Hive
- The difficulty of collecting log in real time
- Troublesome analysis of each service log respectively

In order to solve these problems, the company considered introducing Apache Kafka and Spark. Kafka is a queuing system for big data conveying (see Figure 6-11). Kafka does not process or transform each data itself. Kafka made it possible to convey a lot of data from a data center to other data centers reliably. So it is a required platform to construct pipeline architecture at a huge scale.

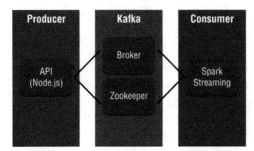

Figure 6-11: The architecture overview of Kafka and Spark streaming

Kafka has a unit called topic whose offset and replication are managed. By using topic and a group of readers called ConsumerGroup, we can obtain the log unit that is separated by service type. In order to do real-time processing, we adapt Spark streaming that is a stream processing module in Spark. Spark streaming is a micro batch framework to be exact. Micro batch framework divides a stream into the mini collection of data. A normal batch process is applied toward the mini collection. So in terms of the algorithm of processing, there is no difference between batch processing and micro-batch processing. This is one of the reasons why we adapted Spark streaming rather than other streaming processing platforms such as Storm or Samza. We can easily convert current logic toward Spark streaming. Thanks to introducing this architecture, we could achieve the results below.

- **Managing the termination of each data with Kafka**. Kafka deletes expired unnecessary data automatically. We don't need to pay attention to this anymore.

- **Succeeding to minimize the time to store data into storage** (HBase). We can make it from 2 hours to 10~20 seconds.
- **Reducing the time to visualization** because of converting some processes to Spark streaming. We can also make it from 2 hours to 5 seconds.

Spark streaming is easy to use because the API is almost the same as the one of Spark itself. So a user who is familiar with Scala can easily become used to Spark streaming. And also, Spark streaming can be easily used on a Hadoop platform (YARN) seamlessly. It won't take an hour to construct a cluster that does Spark streaming. But one thing to note here is that Spark streaming occupies CPU and memory for a long time unlike normal Spark jobs. And in order to finish the processing of each data in fixed time reliably, it is necessary to do some tuning. If you cannot achieve very fast streaming processing (sub-second processing) with Spark streaming, we recommend that you consider other platforms such as Storm or Samza.

Real-Time Recommendation with Spark

The most demanding field of machine learning is currently recommendation. You can see a lot of examples of recommendation such as e-commerce, advertisement, and online booking services. We use Spark Streaming and GraphX to make a recommendation system about items we are selling. GraphX is a library for a distributed graph processing library. This library is also developed under a Spark project. We can use RDD called a resilient distributed property graph that extends the original RDD. GraphX provides a basis for the manipulation of the graph, and the API that is similar to the one of Pregel.

The overview of our recommendation system can be written like below. First we collect tweet data from Twitter for each user. Following processing with micro-batch is done by Spark streaming, collecting tweets every five seconds and processing. Since tweets are written in natural language (in this case, Japanese), we need to separate each word with morphological analysis. In the second phase we use Kuromoji to do this separation. In order to make a relation to our item database, it was necessary to create a user defined dictionary for Kuromoji. This is the most important point to achieve a meaningful recommendation (see Figure 6-12).

At the third phase, we made a score for the relationship between each word and item. We had to also tune our user defined dictionary to make the relevance between each word and item nicer. In particular, we removed nonalphabetical characters and added adhoc relevant words. After this phase we can obtain a collection of words from each tweet. But this collection includes several irrelevant words for our items. So at the fourth phase, we use SVM to filter related words to our items. We trained SVM as supervised learning; label 0 represents non-related tweets; label 1 represents related tweets. After creating this supervised learning data, we trained the model. Then we can only extract related tweets from raw data. The last step is for analyzing the relevance between items and words. If clustering succeeds, we can recommend another item in the same cluster to a user (see Figure 6-13).

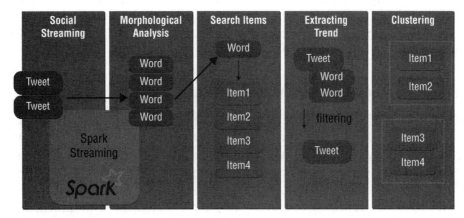

Figure 6-12: Spark streaming

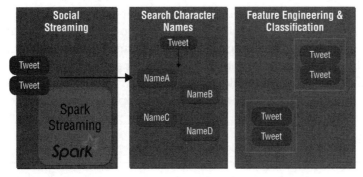

Figure 6-13: Spark streaming analyzes the relevance of words

Though the main trouble to note is creating the user defined dictionary, there are several points to write here about Spark streaming.

- `Map#filterKeys` and `Map#mapValues not serializable`—We could not use these transformations in Scala 2.10. Since Spark 1.1 depends on Scala 2.10, we could not use these functions. This is already solved with Scala 2.11.

- Restricted output operation of `DStream`—There are not so many output operations in current `DStream`. `print`, `saveAsTextFiles`, `saveAsObjectFiles`, `saveAsHadoopFiles`, `foreachRDD`. On the other methods, we can not do any operations with side effects. For example, `println` had no effect on map function. It made debugging difficult.

■ Cannot create new RDD in `StreamContext`—`DStream` as a continuous sequence of RDD. We can easily separate or transform the initial RDD, but it was difficult to create a totally new RDD inside StreamContext.

In this system, we used Spark streaming, GraphX, and Spark MLlib. Although we also used Solr as a search engine, almost all functionalities were covered by Spark libraries. This is one of the strongest characteristics of Spark that other frameworks cannot take in the same way yet.

Real-Time Categorization of Twitter Bots

This might be a kind of hobby project. So please feel free to read the last section of this book comfortably. We've done an analysis of a twitter bot of game characters and visualized the relationships between each bot account. Similar to previous examples, we used Spark streaming for collecting tweet data. The character names can have orthographical variants. So we converted unique names in tweets by using the search engine, Solr. The main advantage of Spark streaming, we felt in this example, was that Spark streaming had already implemented machine learning algorithms (MLlib) or graph algorithms (GraphX). So we could analyze tweets immediately without preparing other libraries or writing algorithms. But we faced the problem of the lack of data to show some meaningful visualization. In addition to this, it was difficult to extract meaningful features from each tweet content. This might be caused by the lack of tweet data that is due to the fact that we currently searched the Twitter accounts manually. Specifically, Spark streaming is a scalable system that can process huge data sets. We felt we should utilize the power of scalability of Spark.

Summary

In this chapter, we explained ecosystem libraries that are developed by the Spark core community. And we introduced concrete usage of Spark libraries for ML/MLlib and Spark Streaming. Various use cases and frameworks that are useful for enterprise usage were introduced in this chapter. We hope that this introduction can be a help to your workload development or making business decisions of your daily work. Spark can broadly apply various types of use cases. This is achieved by the flexible architecture of Spark itself, and a lot of ecosystem frameworks provided by the community. We can see the activity of a Spark community from the number of packages registered in `spark-packages.org`. Currently, on Dec 16, 2015, 161 packages were already registered. One year has passed since `spark-packages.org` was released. So we can know there are amazing numbers of community libraries that are developed and maintained by the Spark community (see Figure 6-14).

Community Growth

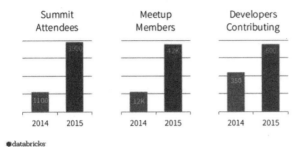

Figure 6-14: **Figure 6-14:** Evolving Spark

http://www.slideshare.net/databricks/spark-summit-eu-2015-matei-zaharia-keynote/3

The Spark community is a thriving open source community. At the last part, We want to note one final thing about active development. Spark communties are subject to be changed anytime in the near future. So please keep up with the latest information if you want to use it in your production usage.

Index